Keto Holiday Cookbook

Delicious Cookbook with Low-Carb Holiday Recipes for the Festive Season to Include Thanksgiving and Christmas.

Contents

Introduction

Winter holidays come with a whole new level of excitement and fun. Everyone anticipates the magical celebrations as these holidays bring everyone closer and provide us a perfect chance to share the warmth and love we have for one another. Serving delicious meals at the tables and sharing drinks are some of the holiday traditions that never get old. Every winter holiday and occasion calls for special meals and dishes, which add to the significance of the event. Whether it's Thanksgiving or Christmas, New Year, or Hanukkah, we all want to enjoy the traditional dishes that are associated with these occasions. And when all these special dishes are cooked at home, they taste more delectable because of all the love you add to every ounce of your meal. For a ketogenic dieter, enjoying the same traditional recipes can be troublesome as they need to maintain their carb intake all the time. This cookbook comes as a holiday gift for all the low-carb eaters who want to enjoy the same delicious recipe but with minimum carbs. This *Keto Holiday Recipes Cookbook* is full of all the traditional recipes and is created by keeping the ketogenic approach in mind. Before you dive in, let's see what type of holiday recipes you should expect in this cookbook.

Special Menus for Winter Holidays

Every winter holiday has a menu of its own, and without this menu, it seems like the celebrations are almost incomplete. For instance, Thanksgiving does not seem complete without a nicely roasted turkey on the dinner table. Or Christmas won't feel special if you don't get to drink the classic eggnog with your friends on the eve. From all the given recipes in this cookbook, you can create your very own winter holiday menu. Try to mix and match different recipes from different sections—pair a delicious dip or spread to serve with your roasted turkey crown, add a rich salad and low-carb dessert to complete your menu, etc. The book is divided into two different parts according to the two main holidays of the winter season. The first part is all about the Thanksgiving recipes, and the second part is about the Christmas recipes. These parts are further divided into chapters to share more of the low-carb recipes according to each occasion. Here is what you can find in this cookbook:

Thanksgiving Turkeys

From butter-basted roasted turkey to rich stuffed turkeys, here you can find them all. Turkey crown and turkey breast recipes are also shared in the first part of the cookbook.

Chicken and Duck Roast

You'll find a variety of chicken and duck roast recipes that you can try as a perfect alternative to turkeys for Thanksgiving celebrations.

Cheesy Casseroles and Sides

If you like to serve heart-melting casseroles for special dinners, then you can find some great low-carb options here. There is also a variety of sides and salad recipes to serve on these occasions.

Dips and Salsa

A festive dinner is incomplete without serving dips and salsas on the side, so we bring you some of the best low-carb dips and salsa for the holidays.

Warming Drinks

Then there are healthy drinks that you can try for the Christmas holidays.

Before going any further, let us rewind and review the ketogenic approach so that people who are new to this diet can have a better understanding of the dos and don'ts of this low-carb high-fat diet to prepare their mind and holiday pantry accordingly in light of these keto facts:

Quick Keto Fact Checks

Back in the 1900s, the ketogenic diet came to be used as a natural therapy for epilepsy, a brain-related disease. Later it was acknowledged for many of its other long-lasting health benefits. The word *ketogenic* is derived from the process called *ketosis*. It is a metabolic process in which ketones and a large amount of energy are produced by the breakdown of fat, in the absence of carbohydrates. For a meal to be termed as keto, it should not have more than 15 grams of carbohydrates per serving. Food items containing carbs have to be avoided; these include all sugars, wheat, grains, lentils, milk, high-carb fruits, and vegetables. Contrary to this, all fat-rich ingredients are completely permissible on a ketogenic diet. With this, regular exercise and a balanced approach are also quite important. Ketosis can only take place in the absence of glucose—a basic carbohydrate. In this process, energy is released through the breakdown of fats instead of carbohydrates, and the byproducts are ketones. A well-balanced ketogenic plan is important to gain the benefits of ketosis. Any imbalance can lead to ketoacidosis, which is fatal in extreme cases. Ketoacidosis can be a problem specifically for people with type 1 diabetes. So, they need to be extra careful. Therefore, it is always recommended to consult a health expert before opting for a ketogenic diet.

As the ketogenic diet puts fat into good use, all the good and bad cholesterols are processed out of the body. The blood cholesterol levels, therefore, drop to a desirable state. Lesser cholesterol in the blood means no accumulation in the vessels, and no obstruction in the cardiovascular system. Since all diabetic patients suffer from high blood sugar levels due to low production of insulin, they can gain maximum benefit out of the ketogenic diet as it provides better low-carb alternatives. They can live an active and healthy life without using any forms of sugar at all.

We all know that a single fat molecule produces twice the amount of energy produced by the breakdown of the same amount of carbohydrates. That is why the ketogenic diet being rich in fat gives a high boost of energy after every single meal. Such energy is enough to spend the day with good zeal. Scientific studies have also recently discovered a direct relation between vitality and ketogenic life by observing people who have been eating keto for years. It can be all true as a balanced diet is a key to longevity, and the keto diet ensures that balance.

As discussed earlier, this diet emerged as a non-medicinal treatment of epilepsy, which proves its effectiveness in improving mental health. Doctors are now even prescribing it to Alzheimer's patients as a long-lasting treatment. Both energy and fat from the keto diet are responsible for strengthening our brain cells. We have already established the fact that the ketogenic diet helps to remove fat deposits from the body. Eventually, it reduces obesity. Within two to three weeks of a keto lifestyle, two or three pounds can be lost. High energy equals an active metabolism since the ketogenic diet ensures a high amount of energy; it accelerates our rate of metabolism to a great extent.

What Can You Eat on a Ketogenic Diet?

➢ Meaty Treats

Meat in any of its forms doesn't contain carbohydrates, so it is completely allowed on a ketogenic diet. It includes seafood, chicken, turkey, duck, beef, mutton, lamb, pork, etc.

➢ Keto-Specific Vegetables

Keto-friendly vegetables include green leafy vegetables, tomatoes, cucumber, asparagus, broccoli, cabbage, cauliflower, etc.

➢ Seeds and Nuts

Seeds and dry nuts do not contain excessive carbohydrates, and a balanced amount of them can be eaten on a keto diet. Pumpkin seeds, pistachios, almonds, etc., are all allowed.

➢ Dairy Items

For dairy products, we need to be a bit more careful as not all of them are prohibited on a keto diet. Milk contains more carbohydrates; therefore, it should be avoided. Whereas cheese, yogurt, cream, cream cheese, butter, and eggs are all keto-friendly.

Animal milk can be substituted with:

1. Almond milk

2. Soy milk

3. Coconut milk

4. Macadamia milk

5. Hemp milk

➢ **Ketogenic Fruits**

Like veggies, not all fruits are good for the ketogenic diet. Some are high in carbs like apples, pineapples, bananas, etc. However, you can enjoy blackberries, cranberries, avocado, coconut, blueberries, and strawberries, as they have a low-carb content.

➢ **All Fats**

When it comes to fat, there is no compulsion or reservations for a ketogenic diet. You can use all plant oils and animal fat, including olive oil, ghee, canola oil, etc.

➢ **Keto Sweeteners**

Being on a ketogenic diet doesn't mean that you should say goodbye to all desserts. You can also enjoy some sweetness with special sugar substitutes. They do not contain a high level of carbohydrates and still provide good taste. Some of the commonly used substitutes are:

1. Stevia

2. Erythritol

3. Swerve

4. Monk fruit sweetener

5. Natvia

It is important to note here that these sweeteners vary in their level of sweetness and can substitute sugar accordingly. Stevia is two hundred times sweeter than table sugar, so a teaspoon of stevia is enough to replace 1 cup of sugar. However, it is better to use it "to taste." All other keto sweeteners are as equally sweet as the white or brown sugars.

Table 1: Food to Avoid

Fruits	Legumes	Sugars	Grains	Tubers /vegetables	Dairy Products
Apples	Lentils	White	Rice	Yams	Animal Milk
Bananas	Chickpeas	Brown	Wheat	Potatoes	
Pineapples	Black beans	Maple syrup	Corn	Beets	
Oranges	Garbanzo beans	Agave	Barley	Yellow Squash	
Pears	Lima beans	Honey, Molasses	Millet		
Pomegranates	Kidney beans	Confectioner's sugar	Oats		
Watermelon	White beans	Granulated sugar	Quinoa		

What You Should Avoid on a Ketogenic Diet

1. Grains

Edible grains are a great source of carbohydrates, whether it's wheat, rice, barley, millet, etc. So, these all are strictly forbidden on a keto-friendly diet. Products obtained from these grains are also not allowed, including wheat flour, all-purpose flour, rice flours, etc. Flour of such sort can be replaced with:

➢ Almond flour

➢ Coconut flour

2. Legumes

All legumes are grown underground, and they are high-carb food items. Legumes include all lentils, beans, and chickpeas. None of them are keto-friendly and should be completely avoided.

3. Sugar

Sugar is nothing but the purest form of carbohydrates. Hence, it should be avoided completely, whether it's white sugar, confectionary, granulated, brown, baking sugar, etc. Products containing a high level of sugar are also prohibited like molasses, honey, dates, processed food, and beverages.

4. Fruits

Fruits like bananas, oranges, apples, pomegranates, pineapples, pears, and watermelon are all very rich in sugar. Avoid these fruits, especially on a ketogenic diet. Extract and juices obtained from these fruits should be avoided.

5. Tubers

Tubers are underground vegetables, and they basically store food for plants in the form of carbohydrates. These include potatoes, beetroots, and yams. They all are not good for a ketogenic diet.

6. Dairy

All dairy items are allowed on a ketogenic diet except for animal milk.

Table 2: Food To Eat

Fruits	Vegetables	Meat	Nuts	Dairy	Oils
Avocados	Artichoke hearts	Beef	Almonds	Coconut milk	Almond oil
Blueberries	Arugula	Chicken	Brazil nuts	Almond milk	Avocado oil

Coconuts	Asparagus	Pork	Hazelnuts/ filberts	Coconut cream	Cacao butter
Cranberries	Bell peppers	Fish	Macadamia nuts	Butter	Coconut oil
Lemons	Beets	Turkey	Pecans	Cheeses	Flaxseed oil
Limes	Bok choy	Duck	Peanuts	Silken Tofu	Hazelnut oil
Olives	Broccoli	Quail	Pine nuts	Ghee	Macadamia nut oil
Raspberries	Brussels sprouts	Shrimp	Walnuts		MCT oil
Strawberries	Cabbage	Lobster	Chia		Olive oil
Tomatoes	Carrots	Mussels	Hemp		Healthy Oils
	Cauliflower	Prawns	Pumpkin		Almond oil

Part 1: Thanksgiving Recipes

Chapter 1: Keto Main Course Recipes— Turkey

Turkey Mushroom Meatballs

Ingredients

- ➤ 1 pound turkey meat, ground
- ➤ 1 yellow onion, minced
- ➤ 4 garlic cloves, minced
- ➤ ¼ cup parsley, chopped
- ➤ Salt and black pepper, to taste
- ➤ 1 teaspoon oregano, dried
- ➤ 1 egg, whisked
- ➤ ¼ cup almond milk
- ➤ 2 teaspoons coconut aminos

- ➤ 12 mushrooms, chopped
- ➤ 1 cup chicken stock
- ➤ 2 tablespoon olive oil
- ➤ 2 tablespoon ghee

How to prepare

1. Thoroughly mix turkey meat with onion, garlic, parsley, pepper, salt, egg, aminos, and oregano in a bowl.
2. Make small 1-inch meatballs out of this mixture.
3. Add these meatballs along with other ingredients into a cooking pot.
4. Cover the meatballs with a lid and cook for 7 minutes on medium heat.
5. Flip the meatballs and continue cooking for another 7 minutes.
6. Garnish as desired.
7. Serve warm.

Preparation time: 10 minutes
Cooking time: 14 minutes
Total time: 24 minutes
Servings: 8

Nutritional Values

- ➤ *Calories 293*

- *Total Fat 16 g*
- *Saturated Fat 2.3 g*
- *Cholesterol 75 mg*
- *Total Carbs 5.2 g*
- *Sugar 2.6 g*
- *Fiber 1.9 g*
- *Sodium 386 mg*
- *Protein 34.2 g*

Lemon-Garlic Turkey Roast

Ingredients

- 11 pounds whole turkey, neck and giblets removed
- 1 onion, halved
- 1 lemon, halved
- 1 garlic bulb; halved, peeled, and minced

Salt mix

- 2 tablespoons of sea salt

- ➢ 1 tablespoon thyme leaves
- ➢ 1 teaspoon peppercorns

<u>Butter</u>

- ➢ 3 ½ ounces butter
- ➢ 4 tablespoon vegetable bouillon powder
- ➢ 1 lemon, zested

How to prepare

1. Add sea salt, thyme leaves, and peppercorns to a mortar, and blend these ingredients with the pestle.
2. Place the whole turkey on a baking sheet and loosen its skin by pushing your fingers under its skin.
3. Stuff the thyme salt mixture under the skin and marinate the turkey for 2 days in the refrigerator.
4. Mix butter with bouillon powder and lemon zest. And brush this butter mixture on top of the turkey.
5. Now set the oven for preheating at 390°F.
6. Stuff the turkey with lemon halves, garlic, and onion, then roast it for 4 hours in the oven.
7. Carve and serve.

Preparation time: 10 minutes

Cooking time: 4 hours

Total time: 4 hours 10 minutes

Servings: 16

Nutritional Values

- ➢ *Calories 695*
- ➢ *Total Fat 17.5 g*
- ➢ *Saturated Fat 4.8 g*
- ➢ *Cholesterol 283 mg*
- ➢ *Total Carbs 6.4 g*
- ➢ *Fiber 1.8 g*
- ➢ *Sugar 0.8 g*
- ➢ *Sodium 355 mg*
- ➢ *Protein 117.4 g*

Pancetta Shallot-Stuffed Turkey

Ingredients

- ➤ 11 pounds oven-ready turkey, neck and giblets removed
- ➤ 1 pack smoked sliced pancetta
- ➤ 1 tablespoon olive oil

Butter

- ➤ 1 large garlic clove
- ➤ 1 tablespoon thyme leaves

- ➤ 1 lemon, zested
- ➤ 3 ounces butter, softened

Shallots
- ➤ 14 ounces shallots, peeled
- ➤ 1 small handful thyme sprigs
- ➤ 1 handful bay leaves
- ➤ 1 lemon, cut in half

How to prepare

1. Mix butter with lemon zest, thyme leaves, and garlic clove in a bowl.
2. Toss shallots with thyme sprigs, bay leaves, and lemon halves.
3. Place the turkey in a roasting tin, stuff it with pancetta slices, shallots mixture, and brush its top with butter mixture.
4. Now set the oven for preheating at 370°F.
5. Roast the stuffed turkey for 4 hours in the oven.
6. Allow the roasted turkey to rest for 30 minutes then slice to serve.
7. Enjoy.

Preparation time: 10 minutes

Cooking time: 4 hours

Total time: 4 hours 10 minutes

Servings: 12

Nutritional Values

➢ *Calories 215*

➢ *Total Fat 12.5 g*

➢ *Saturated Fat 6.8 g*

➢ *Cholesterol 58 mg*

➢ *Sodium 130 mg*

➢ *Total Carbohydrates 1.9 g*

➢ *Dietary Fiber 0.1 g*

➢ *Sugars 1.8 g*

➢ *Protein 53.9 g*

Herb-Basted Turkey Roast

Ingredients

- ➢ 11 pounds free-range oven-ready turkey
- ➢ 3 ½ ounces butter, softened
- ➢ Zest from 1 lemon
- ➢ 1 tablespoon thyme, chopped
- ➢ 2 tablespoons parsley, chopped
- ➢ 1 garlic clove, finely chopped
- ➢ Hazelnut, pancetta, for stuffing

How to prepare

1. Stuff the turkey with pancetta and hazelnut stuffing.
2. Place it in the roasting tin and rub it with butter, lemon zest, thyme, parsley, and garlic.
3. Now set the oven for preheating at 390°F.
4. Roast the stuffed turkey for 4 hours until golden-brown.
5. Serve warm.

Preparation time: 10 minutes

Cooking time: 4 hours

Total time: 4 hours 10 minutes

Servings: 16

Nutritional Values

➢ *Calories 295*

➢ *Total Fat 18.5 g*

➢ *Saturated Fat 7.8 g*

➢ *Cholesterol 21 mg*

➢ *Sodium 92 mg*

➢ *Total Carbohydrates 2.9 g*

➢ *Dietary Fiber 4 g*

➢ *Sugars 1.6 g*

➢ *Protein 61.3 g*

Sausage-Stuffed Turkey Roast

Ingredients

Stuffing

- ➤ 4 ounces madeira or white wine
- ➤ 2/3 ounce pack dried porcini mushrooms
- ➤ 2 onions, halved and sliced
- ➤ 2 tablespoons butter

- ½ ounce pack thyme, leaves
- 2 x 14 ounces Packs Cumberland sausages, skins removed
- Zest of 1 lemon
- ½ ounce pack flat-leaf parsley, chopped
- 3 ounces almond meal
- 10 rashers streaky bacon

Turkey

- 1 onion, quartered
- 11 pounds bronze turkey, giblets removed
- 3 ounces butter, softened
- 1 whole nutmeg
- 10 rashers streaky bacon
- 4 ounces glass madeira or white wine

How to prepare

Stuffing

1. Mix mushrooms with madeira in a bowl.
2. Sauté onions with butter for 10 minutes in a pan.
3. Add mushrooms with their liquid and thyme leaves.
4. Stir in bacon, almond meal, parsley, and sausage, then sauté for 3 minutes.

Turkey

5. Layer a roasting tin with bacon and place the turkey on top.

6. Stuff the whole turkey with the prepared stuffing and brush it with butter.

7. Drizzle nutmeg and wine on top of the turkey.

8. Now set the oven for preheating at 390°F.

9. Roast the stuffed turkey for 4 hours until golden-brown.

10. Serve warm.

Preparation time: 10 minutes

Cooking time: 4 hours 13 minutes

Total time: 4 hours 23 minutes

Servings: 12

Nutritional Values

➢ *Calories 474*

➢ *Total Fat 8.4 g*

➢ *Saturated Fat 2.4 g*

➢ *Cholesterol 8 mg*

➢ *Sodium 40 mg*

➢ *Total Carbohydrates 2 g*

➢ *Dietary Fiber 1.2 g*

➢ *Sugars 0.1 g*

➢ *Protein 52.2 g*

Herb-Rubbed Turkey Breast

Ingredients

- ➢ 1 (6-pound) whole bone-in turkey breast
- ➢ 1 tablespoon minced garlic
- ➢ 2 teaspoons dry mustard
- ➢ 1 tablespoon fresh rosemary leaves, chopped
- ➢ 1 tablespoon fresh sage leaves, chopped
- ➢ 1 teaspoon fresh thyme leaves, chopped
- ➢ 2 teaspoons kosher salt

- 1 teaspoon freshly ground black pepper
- 2 tablespoons olive oil
- 2 tablespoons lemon juice
- 1 cup dry white wine

How to prepare

1. Set the oven for preheating at 325°F.
2. Place the turkey breast in a roasting pan.
3. Mix wine with the remaining herbs and ingredients.
4. Pour this mixture over the turkey breast and brush it liberally.
5. Roast the turkey breast for 1 hour 30 minutes in the oven.
6. Slice and serve.

Preparation time: 10 minutes

Cooking time: 1 hour 30 minutes

Total time: 1 hour 40 minutes

Servings: 12

Nutritional Values

- *Calories 328*
- *Total Fat 18.4 g*
- *Saturated Fat 8.4 g*
- *Cholesterol 102 mg*
- *Sodium 162 mg*

- *Total Carbohydrates 3.3 g*
- *Dietary Fiber 1.4 g*
- *Sugars 0.3 g*
- *Protein 44.2 g*

Turkey Breast with Blueberry Glaze

Ingredients

- ➢ 2 tablespoons olive oil
- ➢ 1 large onion, sliced
- ➢ 3 rosemary sprigs
- ➢ 1 (3-pound) bone-in turkey breast with skin on
- ➢ Salt and black pepper, to taste

Blueberry Balsamic Glaze Ingredients

➤ 2 cups frozen blueberries

➤ 1⁄2 cup balsamic vinegar

➤ 1 1⁄2 tablespoons whole-grain mustard

➤ 1⁄4 teaspoon salt and black pepper

How to prepare

1. First, set the oven to preheat at 450°F.

2. Place a heavy bottom skillet over medium-high heat and add olive oil.

3. Stir in onion and sauté for 4 minutes until soft and tender.

4. Add rosemary sprigs to the pan then rub the turkey with oil, salt, and black pepper.

5. Set the turkey in the skillet and roast it for 40 minutes in the oven at 400°F.

6. Meanwhile, prepare the blueberry glaze in a saucepan.

7. Add all the ingredients for this glaze to the pan and let the glaze cook on simmer until it is reduced to half.

8. Drizzle the glaze over the turkey breast then continue roasting for another 20 minutes.

9. Slice and serve warm.

Preparation time: 10 minutes

Cooking time: 64 minutes

Total time: 74 minutes

Servings: 6

Nutritional Values

- ➢ *Calories 394*
- ➢ *Total Fat 25.2 g*
- ➢ *Saturated Fat 14.9 g*
- ➢ *Cholesterol 130 mg*
- ➢ *Sodium 210 mg*
- ➢ *Total Carbohydrates 0.3 g*
- ➢ *Dietary Fiber 0.8 g*
- ➢ *Sugars 1.8 g*
- ➢ *Protein 3.9 g*

Thyme Garlic Turkey Crown

Ingredients

- ➢ 1 big bunch thyme
- ➢ 2 garlic cloves
- ➢ 1 lemon, zested and juiced
- ➢ 4 ½ pounds turkey crown
- ➢ 2/3 ounce butter, softened

How to prepare

1. Set the oven for preheating at 375°F.
2. Mix butter with garlic, lemon juice, and zest in a small bowl.
3. Place the turkey crown in a roasting pan.
4. Brush the garlic butter on top and place thyme sprigs over the turkey.
5. Bake it for 1 hour 30 minutes in the preheated oven.
6. Serve warm.

Preparation time: 10 minutes

Cooking time: 1hour 30 minutes

Total time: 1 hour 40 minutes

Servings: 8

Nutritional Values

➢ *Calories 456*
➢ *Total Fat 32.3 g*
➢ *Saturated Fat 17.4 g*
➢ *Cholesterol 122 mg*
➢ *Sodium 379 mg*
➢ *Total Carbohydrates 3 g*
➢ *Dietary Fiber 0.2 g*
➢ *Sugars 2.2 g*
➢ *Protein 57.5 g*

Smoked Turkey Crown

Ingredients

- ➢ 1 tablespoon smoked paprika
- ➢ 1 teaspoon dried herbs
- ➢ 4 ½ pounds turkey crown, on the bone
- ➢ 2/3 ounce butter, softened

How to prepare

1. Set the oven for preheating, at 350°F.

2. Mix butter with all the herbs and spices in a mixing bowl.

3. Place the turkey crown in a roasting pan and pat it dry.

4. Liberally brush the butter mixture over the turkey crown.

5. Roast it for 1 hour 30 minutes in the oven.

6. Serve warm.

Preparation time: 10 minutes

Cooking time: 1 hour 30 minutes

Total time: 1 hour 40 minutes

Servings: 8

Nutritional Values

➢ *Calories 269*

➢ *Total Fat 13.7 g*

➢ *Saturated Fat 6.7 g*

➢ *Cholesterol 53 mg*

➢ *Sodium 38 mg*

➢ *Total Carbohydrates 3.1 g*

➢ *Dietary Fiber 0.8 g*

➢ *Sugars 1.2 g*

➢ *Protein 45.1 g*

Basic Turkey Meatloaf

Ingredients

- ➤ 1 2/3 pounds ground turkey
- ➤ ½ cup almond milk
- ➤ 1 small onion, chopped
- ➤ 1 egg
- ➤ 1½ teaspoons salt
- ➤ 2 garlic cloves, minced
- ➤ ¼ teaspoon ground black pepper

➤ 2 tablespoons sugar-free ketchup

How to prepare

1. Set the oven for preheating at 350°F.
2. Mix all the ingredients for turkey meatloaf in a mixing bowl.
3. Spread this mixture in a suitable greased loaf pan.
4. Bake the turkey meatloaf for 30 minutes in the preheated oven.
5. Brush the sugar-free ketchup on top of the meatloaf.
6. Then bake again for 30 minutes, then slice.
7. Serve warm.

Preparation time: 10 minutes

Cooking time: 60 minutes

Total time: 70 minutes

Servings: 6

Nutritional Values

➤ *Calories 400*
➤ *Total Fat 16.8 g*
➤ *Saturated Fat 6.9 g*
➤ *Cholesterol 76 mg*
➤ *Sodium 304 mg*
➤ *Total Carbohydrates 5.7 g*

➢ *Dietary Fiber 1.4 g*

➢ *Sugars 1.2 g*

➢ *Protein 65.6 g*

Chapter 2: Keto Main Course Recipes— Turkey Alternatives

Saucy Gingered Duck

Ingredients

➢ 1 (4-pound) duck, cut into pieces

- ➢ 2 tablespoons ginger garlic paste
- ➢ 2 green onions, roughly chopped
- ➢ 4 tablespoons soy sauce
- ➢ 4 tablespoons sherry wine
- ➢ Salt and black pepper, to taste

How to prepare

1. Set the oven for preheating at 350°F.
2. Start by tossing the duck with all other ingredients in a bowl.
3. Marinate the meat for 4 hours in the refrigerator.
4. Spread the duck chunks in a baking tray.
5. Bake the meat for 45 minutes with occasional tossing.
6. Serve fresh.

Preparation time: 10 minutes

Cooking time: 15 minutes

Total time: 25 minutes

Servings: 8

Nutritional Values

- ➢ *Calories 225*
- ➢ *Total Fat 14.3 g*
- ➢ *Saturated Fat 0.6 g*
- ➢ *Cholesterol 137 mg*

- ➤ *Sodium 538 mg*
- ➤ *Total Carbs 2.8 g*
- ➤ *Fiber 7 g*
- ➤ *Sugar 0.3 g*
- ➤ *Protein 28.2 g*

Cajun-Rubbed Chicken Thigh

Ingredients

- ➤ 1 pound chicken thighs, cut into halves
- ➤ ¼ cup 1 tablespoon vegetable oil
- ➤ ½ cup almond flour
- ➤ 1 cup vegetable stock
- ➤ 1 teaspoon Cajun spice

➢ Salt and black pepper, to taste

How to prepare

1. Start by tossing the chicken with salt, black pepper, and 1 tablespoon oil in a bowl.
2. Cover the thighs and refrigerate for 1 hour for marination.
3. Sear the marinated chicken in a sauté pan.
4. Cook chicken for 5 minutes per side until golden-brown.
5. Whisk almond flour with Cajun spice and remaining oil in a separate bowl.
6. Add almond mixture to a cooking pot and stir for 2 minutes.
7. Stir in stock and cook well until it thickens.
8. Toss in the sear chicken and cook for 4 minutes.
9. Serve fresh and warm.

Preparation time: 10 minutes
Cooking time: 16 minutes
Total time: 26 minutes
Servings: 2

Nutritional Values

➢ *Calories 433*
➢ *Total Fat 15.2 g*

- ➤ *Saturated Fat 8.6 g*
- ➤ *Cholesterol 179 mg*
- ➤ *Sodium 318 mg*
- ➤ *Total Carbs 2.7 g*
- ➤ *Fiber 1.1 g*
- ➤ *Sugar 1.1 g*
- ➤ *Protein 68.4 g*

Spicy Chicken Breasts

Ingredients

- ➢ 1 pound chicken breast, skinless and boneless
- ➢ 1 cup chunky salsa
- ➢ ¾ teaspoon cumin
- ➢ A pinch of oregano
- ➢ Salt and black pepper, to taste

How to prepare

1. Pat dry the chicken and rub it with salt and pepper.
2. Set a suitable cooking pot over medium heat.
3. Place the chicken breast in the pot and top them with cumin, oregano, and salsa.
4. Cover the lid and cook the chicken for 20 minutes on a simmer.
5. Serve the chicken meat with its salsa.
6. Enjoy.

Preparation time: 10 minutes

Cooking time: 20 minutes

Total time: 30 minutes

Servings: 2

Nutritional Values

- *Calories 272*
- *Total Fat 27 g*
- *Saturated Fat 16 g*
- *Cholesterol 83 mg*
- *Sodium 175 mg*
- *Total Carbs 7.8 g*
- *Fiber 0.4 g*
- *Sugar 5.2 g*
- *Protein 5.3 g*

Italian Dijon Chicken

Ingredients

- ➤ 2 pounds chicken thighs, skinless and boneless
- ➤ ¼ cup lemon juice
- ➤ 2 tablespoons olive oil
- ➤ 3 tablespoons Dijon mustard
- ➤ 2 tablespoons Italian seasoning
- ➤ Salt and black pepper, to taste

How to prepare

1. Start by tossing chicken with all other ingredients in a bowl.

2. Prepare and preheat the grill on medium heat.

3. Grill the chicken pieces for 5 minutes per side until al dente.

4. Serve fresh.

Preparation time: 10 minutes

Cooking time: 10 minutes

Total time: 20 minutes

Servings: 4

Nutritional Values

- ➤ *Calories 242*
- ➤ *Total Fat 15.9 g*
- ➤ *Saturated Fat 10.6 g*
- ➤ *Cholesterol 36 mg*
- ➤ *Sodium 421 mg*
- ➤ *Total Carbs 4.6 g*
- ➤ *Fiber 2 g*
- ➤ *Sugar 1.6 g*
- ➤ *Protein 20.8 g*

Chicken Carrot Medley

Ingredients

- ➤ 6 chicken thighs
- ➤ 15 ounces canned tomatoes, chopped.
- ➤ 1 yellow onion, chopped.
- ➤ 2 cups chicken stock
- ➤ ¼ pound baby carrots, cut into halves
- ➤ Salt and black pepper, to taste

How to prepare

1. Start by adding chicken and all other ingredients to a suitable cooking pot.

2. Cover the pot's lid and cook for 30 minutes on medium-low heat.

3. Mix well and serve fresh.

Preparation time: 10 minutes

Cooking time: 30 minutes

Total time: 40 minutes

Servings: 6

Nutritional Values

➤ *Calories 362*

➤ *Total Fat 15.9 g*

➤ *Saturated Fat 9.9 g*

➤ *Cholesterol 49 mg*

➤ *Sodium 684 mg*

➤ *Total Carbs 4.1 g*

➤ *Fiber 1.4 g*

➤ *Sugar 1.1 g*

➤ *Protein 23.3 g*

Chicken Tomatillos

Ingredients

- ➤ 1 pound chicken thighs, skinless and boneless
- ➤ 2 tablespoons extra-virgin olive oil
- ➤ 1 yellow onion, thinly sliced
- ➤ 5 ounces tomatoes, chopped.
- ➤ Salt and black pepper, to taste
- ➤ 15 ounces canned tomatillos, chopped.

How to prepare

1. Start by heating olive oil in a cooking pot.
2. Toss in chicken, tomatillos, onion, salt, pepper, and tomatoes.
3. Cook for 15 minutes on medium-low heat and cover the pot with the lid.
4. Stir well and serve fresh.

Preparation time: 10 minutes

Cooking time: 15 minutes

Total time: 25 minutes

Servings: 4

Nutritional Values

- ➢ *Calories 260*
- ➢ *Total Fat 13 g*
- ➢ *Saturated Fat 5 g*
- ➢ *Cholesterol 0.3 mg*
- ➢ *Sodium 465 mg*
- ➢ *Total Carbs 6 g*
- ➢ *Fiber 5.4 g*
- ➢ *Sugar 1.3 g*
- ➢ *Protein 26 g*

Crispy Italian Chicken

Ingredients

- ➢ 6 chicken thighs
- ➢ 1 cup almond flour
- ➢ 2 eggs, whisked
- ➢ Salt and black pepper, to taste

How to prepare

1. Start by tossing the flour with salt and black pepper on a flat plate.
2. Whisk the eggs in a separate bowl.

3. Coat the chicken thighs with the flour, then dip in the eggs and then coat with flour again.

4. Prepare and preheat the grill on medium heat.

5. Grill the chicken for 5 minutes per side on medium heat.

6. Serve fresh and warm.

Preparation time: 10 minutes

Cooking time: 10 minutes

Total time: 20 minutes

Servings: 6

Nutritional Values

- ➤ *Calories 355*
- ➤ *Total Fat 16.8 g*
- ➤ *Saturated Fat 4 g*
- ➤ *Cholesterol 150 mg*
- ➤ *Sodium 719 mg*
- ➤ *Total Carbs 1.4 g*
- ➤ *Fiber 0.5 g*
- ➤ *Sugar 0.1 g*
- ➤ *Protein 47 g*

Cacciatore Chicken Drumsticks

Ingredients

- ➢ 28 ounces canned tomatoes and juice, crushed.
- ➢ 8 chicken drumsticks, bone-in
- ➢ ½ cup olives, pitted and sliced
- ➢ 1 cup chicken stock
- ➢ 1 yellow onion, chopped.

➢ Salt and black pepper, to taste

How to prepare

1. Start by adding chicken and all other ingredients to a suitable cooking pot.
2. Cover the pot with its lid and cook for 20 minutes with occasional stirring.
3. Serve warm and fresh.

Preparation time: 10 minutes
Cooking time: 20 minutes
Total time: 30 minutes
Servings: 8

Nutritional Values

➢ *Calories 489*
➢ *Total Fat 18.7 g*
➢ *Saturated Fat 3.8 g*
➢ *Cholesterol 151 mg*
➢ *Sodium 636 mg*
➢ *Total Carbs 6.1 g*
➢ *Fiber 0.5 g*
➢ *Sugar 4.3 g*
➢ *Protein 50 g*

Duck Carrot Stew

Ingredients

- ➢ 1 duck, cut into large pieces
- ➢ 2 carrots, chopped
- ➢ 2 cups of water
- ➢ 1 onion, diced
- ➢ 1-inch ginger pieces, chopped
- ➢ Salt and black pepper, to taste

How to prepare

1. Place the duck pieces in a suitable cooking pot

2. Add carrots, wine, onion, ginger, water, salt, and pepper.

3. Mix well and cover duck with the lid.

4. Cook the duck stew for 1 hour on a simmer until the duck is cooked well.

5. Serve warm and fresh.

Preparation time: 10 minutes

Cooking time: 1 hour

Total time: 1 hour 10 minutes

Servings: 8

Nutritional Values

- ➢ *Calories 325*
- ➢ *Total Fat 14.4 g*
- ➢ *Saturated Fat 3.5 g*
- ➢ *Cholesterol 135 mg*
- ➢ *Sodium 552 mg*
- ➢ *Total Carbs 2.3 g*
- ➢ *Fiber 0.4 g*
- ➢ *Sugar 0.5 g*
- ➢ *Protein 44 g*

Chicken Eggplant Mix

Ingredients

- 8 chicken pieces
- 1 eggplant, cubed
- 3 garlic cloves, crushed
- 14 ounces canned coconut milk
- 2 tablespoons green curry paste
- Salt and black pepper, to taste

How to prepare

1. Start by adding chicken and all other ingredients to a

cooking pot.

2. Cover the pot with its lid and cook for 15 minutes with occasional stirring.

3. Serve warm and fresh.

Preparation time: 10 minutes

Cooking time: 15 minutes

Total time: 25 minutes

Servings: 4

Nutritional Values

➢ *Calories 452*

➢ *Total Fat 3.5 g*

➢ *Saturated Fat 0.5 g*

➢ *Cholesterol 181 mg*

➢ *Sodium 461 mg*

➢ *Total Carbs 7.5 g*

➢ *Fiber 1.7 g*

➢ *Sugar 1.3 g*

➢ *Protein 91.8 g*

Chapter 3: Keto Side Dish Recipes

Mayo Eggplant Salad

Ingredients

- ➤ 1 cup of water
- ➤ 3 eggplant, peeled and cubed
- ➤ 3 large eggs; boiled, peeled, and cubed
- ➤ 1/8 cup onion, finely chopped

- ½ cup mayonnaise
- 1 tablespoon fresh parsley, finely chopped
- ½ tablespoon dill pickle juice
- ½ tablespoon mustard
- Salt and black pepper, to taste

How to prepare

1. Start by putting eggplant and water into a suitable cooking pot.
2. Cover the pot with its lid and cook the eggplant for 15 minutes until they are soft.
3. Toss the cooked eggplant with the remaining ingredients in a salad bowl.
4. Mix well and garnish as desired.
5. Serve warm.

Preparation time: 10 minutes
Cooking time: 15 minutes
Total time: 25 minutes
Servings: 8

Nutritional Values

- *Calories 114*
- *Total Fat 9.6 g*
- *Saturated Fat 4.5 g*

- *Cholesterol 10 mg*
- *Total Carbs 3.1 g*
- *Sugar 1.4 g*
- *Fiber 1.5 g*
- *Sodium 155 mg*
- *Protein 3.5 g*

Spiced Carrots

Ingredients

- ½ cup avocado oil
- 3 pounds carrots, sliced
- 1 teaspoon onion powder
- 2 teaspoons garlic powder
- 2 teaspoons sea salt
- ½ teaspoon paprika
- ½ teaspoon ground black pepper
- 2 cups chicken broth

How to prepare

1. Start by putting all the carrots and other ingredients into a suitable cooking pot.

2. Cover the pot with its lid and cook for 5 minutes with occasional stirring.

3. Once done, remove the lid carefully.

4. Mix well and garnish as desired.

5. Serve warm.

Preparation time: 10 minutes

Cooking time: 5 minutes

Total time: 15 minutes

Servings: 8

Nutritional Values

- ➢ *Calories 252*
- ➢ *Total Fat 17.3 g*
- ➢ *Saturated Fat 11.5 g*
- ➢ *Cholesterol 141 mg*
- ➢ *Total Carbs 7.2 g*
- ➢ *Sugar 0.3 g*
- ➢ *Fiber 1.4 g*
- ➢ *Sodium 153 mg*
- ➢ *Protein 5.2 g*

Brussels Sprouts Quinoa Salad

Ingredients

- ➢ ½ cup cabbage, chopped
- ➢ ½ cup quinoa, rinsed
- ➢ ½ carrot, peeled and cut into chunks
- ➢ ¾ cup of water
- ➢ ¼ teaspoon salt

- 1 cup Brussels sprouts, diced
- ½ cup red onions, sliced
- 1 tablespoon brown swerve
- 2 tablespoons balsamic vinegar
- 1 tablespoon vegetable oil
- 1 tablespoon sunflower seeds
- 1 teaspoon ginger, grated
- 1 garlic clove, minced
- Black pepper, to taste

How to prepare

1. Start by putting quinoa and water into a suitable cooking pot.
2. Cover the pot with its lid and cook for 10 minutes or more until quinoa is completely cooked.
3. Strain the cooked quinoa and add to a salad bowl.
4. Toss in all other ingredients and give it a stir.
5. Mix well and garnish as desired.
6. Serve warm

Preparation time: 10 minutes
Cooking time: 10 minutes
Total time: 20 minutes
Servings: 6

Nutritional Values

- ➤ *Calories 195*
- ➤ *Total Fat 14.3 g*
- ➤ *Saturated Fat 10.5 g*
- ➤ *Cholesterol 175 mg*
- ➤ *Total Carbs 4.5 g*
- ➤ *Sugar 0.5 g*
- ➤ *Fiber 0.3 g*
- ➤ *Sodium 125 mg*
- ➤ *Protein 3.2 g*

Saucy Green Beans

Ingredients

- ➢ 1 cup green beans
- ➢ ½ cup bacon, diced
- ➢ ¼ medium onion, diced
- ➢ ½ teaspoon of sea salt
- ➢ ½ teaspoon pepper
- ➢ ½ teaspoon dry mustard
- ➢ ½ tablespoon Worcestershire sauce

- ➤ ½ tablespoon balsamic vinegar
- ➤ 3 tablespoons tomato paste
- ➤ 3 tablespoons dark brown swerve
- ➤ ½ cup chicken stock
- ➤ ½ cup of water

How to prepare

1. Start by adding green beans and all the ingredients into a suitable cooking pot.
2. Cover the pot with its lid and cook the greens for 10 minutes with occasional stirring.
3. Once done, remove the lid of the pot carefully.
4. Mix well and garnish as desired.
5. Serve warm.

Preparation time: 10 minutes
Cooking time: 10 minutes
Total time: 20 minutes
Servings: 4

Nutritional Values

- ➤ *Calories 151*
- ➤ *Total Fat 14.7 g*
- ➤ *Saturated Fat 1.5 g*
- ➤ *Cholesterol 13 mg*

- *Total Carbs 1.5 g*
- *Sugar 0.3 g*
- *Fiber 0.1 g*
- *Sodium 53 mg*
- *Protein 0.8 g*

Carrot Quinoa Salad

Ingredients

- ➤ ½ cup quinoa, rinsed
- ➤ ¾ cup water
- ➤ ¼ teaspoon salt
- ➤ ½ carrot, peeled and shredded
- ➤ ½ cucumber, chopped
- ➤ ½ cup frozen edamame, thawed
- ➤ 3 green onions, chopped

- ➢ 1 cup red cabbage, shredded
- ➢ ½ tablespoon soy sauce
- ➢ 1 tablespoon lime juice
- ➢ 2 tablespoons swerve
- ➢ 1 tablespoon vegetable oil
- ➢ 1 tablespoon freshly grated ginger
- ➢ 1 tablespoon sesame oil
- ➢ Pinch of red pepper flakes
- ➢ ½ cup peanuts, chopped

How to prepare

1. Start by putting quinoa and water into a suitable cooking pot.
2. Cover the pot with its lid and cook for 10 minutes or more until quinoa is completely cooked.
3. Strain the cooked quinoa and add to a salad bowl.
4. Toss in all other ingredients and give it a stir.
5. Mix well and garnish as desired.
6. Serve warm.

Preparation time: 10 minutes

Cooking time: 10 minutes

Total time: 20 minutes

Servings: 6

Nutritional Values

- ➤ *Calories 261*
- ➤ *Total Fat 27.1 g*
- ➤ *Saturated Fat 23.4 g*
- ➤ *Cholesterol 0 mg*
- ➤ *Total Carbs 6.1 g*
- ➤ *Sugar 2.1 g*
- ➤ *Fiber 3.9 g*
- ➤ *Sodium 10 mg*
- ➤ *Protein 1.8 g*

Zucchini'ghetti

Ingredients

- ➤ 2 pounds zucchini, spiralized
- ➤ 2 cup water
- ➤ Cilantro to serve

How to prepare

1. Start by putting zucchini and water into a suitable

cooking pot.

2. Cover the pot with its lid and cook for 10 minutes or more until zucchinis completely cooked.

3. Strain the cooked zucchini and add to a serving bowl.

4. Garnish spaghetti with cilantro.

5. Serve warm.

Preparation time: 10 minutes

Cooking time: 10 minutes

Total time: 20 minutes

Servings: 4

Nutritional Values

➢ *Calories 139*

➢ *Total Fat 4.6 g*

➢ *Saturated Fat 0.5 g*

➢ *Cholesterol 1.2 mg*

➢ *Total Carbs 7.5 g*

➢ *Sugar 6.3 g*

➢ *Fiber 0.6 g*

➢ *Sodium 83 mg*

➢ *Protein 3.8 g*

Chicken Nacho Dip

Ingredients

- ➢ 1 (14-ounce) can diced tomatoes, drained
- ➢ 1 (1-pound) loaf processed cheese, cubed
- ➢ 2 cooked boneless chicken breast halves, shredded
- ➢ 1/3 cup sour cream
- ➢ ¼ cup green onion, diced
- ➢ 1 ½ tablespoons taco seasoning mix
- ➢ 2 tablespoons jalapeno pepper, minced

How to prepare

1. Add all the nacho dip ingredients to a suitable mixing bowl.
2. Mix well and garnish as desired.
3. Serve warm.

Preparation time: 10 minutes
Cooking time: 0 minutes
Total time: 10 minutes
Servings: 8

Nutritional Values

- ➢ *Calories 173*
- ➢ *Total Fat 16.2 g*
- ➢ *Saturated Fat 9.8 g*
- ➢ *Cholesterol 100 mg*
- ➢ *Total Carbs 9.4 g*
- ➢ *Sugar 0.2 g*
- ➢ *Fibre1 g*
- ➢ *Sodium 42 mg*
- ➢ *Protein 33.3 g*

Barbecue Smokies

Ingredients

- ➢ 1 (18-ounce) bottle barbeque sauce
- ➢ 1 cup sugar-free tomato sauce
- ➢ 1 tablespoon Worcestershire sauce
- ➢ 1/3 cup onion, chopped
- ➢ 2 (16-ounce) packages little wieners

How to prepare

1. Start by putting all the smokies ingredients into a suitable cooking pot.

2. Cook them for 15 minutes with occasional stirring.

3. Mix well and garnish as desired.

4. Serve warm.

Preparation time: 10 minutes

Cooking time: 15minutes

Total time: 25 minutes

Servings: 6

Nutritional Values

- ➢ *Calories 251*
- ➢ *Total Fat 24.5 g*
- ➢ *Saturated Fat 14.7 g*
- ➢ *Cholesterol 165 mg*
- ➢ *Total Carbs 4.3 g*
- ➢ *Sugar 0.5 g*
- ➢ *Fiber 1 g*
- ➢ *Sodium 142 mg*
- ➢ *Protein 51.9 g*

Marinated Mushrooms

Ingredients

- ➤ 4 cubes chicken bouillon
- ➤ 4 cubes beef bouillon
- ➤ 2 cups boiling water
- ➤ 1 cup dry red wine
- ➤ 1 teaspoon dill weed
- ➤ 1 teaspoon Worcestershire sauce
- ➤ 1 teaspoon garlic powder

- 4 pounds fresh mushrooms
- ½ cup butter, or more as needed

How to prepare

1. Toss mushrooms with Worcestershire sauce, wine, and garlic powder in a suitable bowl.
2. Cover mushrooms and marinate them for 15 minutes.
3. Transfer the mushrooms along with their marinade to a suitable cooking pot.
4. Stir in the remaining ingredients and cover with the lid to cook for 15 minutes.
5. Mix well and garnish as desired.
6. Serve warm.

Preparation time: 10 minutes
Cooking time: 15 minutes
Total time: 25 minutes
Servings: 8

Nutritional Values

- *Calories 159*
- *Total Fat 34 g*
- *Saturated Fat 10.3 g*
- *Cholesterol 112 mg*
- *Total Carbs 8.5 g*

- *Sugar 2 g*
- *Fiber 1.3 g*
- *Sodium 92 mg*
- *Protein 7.5 g*

Cinnamon Carrots

Ingredients

- ➢ 2 pounds small carrots
- ➢ ½ cup butter, melted
- ➢ ¼ cup packed brown swerve
- ➢ 1 teaspoon vanilla extract
- ➢ ½ teaspoon ground cinnamon
- ➢ ¼ teaspoon salt
- ➢ 1/8 teaspoon ground nutmeg

- ➢ 2 tablespoons water
- ➢ Toasted chopped pecans, optional

How to prepare

1. Toss carrots with all the ingredients in a suitable cooking pot.
2. Cook the carrots on medium heat for 10 minutes with occasional stirring.
3. Mix well and garnish as desired.
4. Serve warm.

Preparation time: 10 minutes

Cooking time: 10 minutes

Total time: 20 minutes

Servings: 4

Nutritional Values

- ➢ *Calories 220*
- ➢ *Total Fat 20.1 g*
- ➢ *Saturated Fat 7.4 g*
- ➢ *Cholesterol 132 mg*
- ➢ *Total Carbs 3 g*
- ➢ *Sugar 0.4 g*
- ➢ *Fiber 2.4 g*
- ➢ *Sodium 157 mg*
- ➢ *Protein 6.1 g*

Chapter 4: Keto Dessert Recipes

Strawberry-Vanilla Ice Cream

Ingredients

- ➤ 1 cup heavy whipping cream
- ➤ 1/3 cup erythritol

- ➢ 3 large egg yolks
- ➢ ½ teaspoon vanilla extract
- ➢ 1 cup strawberries, pureed

How to prepare

1. Add cream to a pot and place it over low heat and warm it up.
2. Stir in 1/3 cup erythritol and mix well to dissolve.
3. Beat in yolks and continue whisking until fluffy.
4. Stir in vanilla extract and mix well until smooth.
5. Mix well together then transfer the mixture to the ice cream machine and churn as per machine's instructions.
6. Freeze it for 1 hour then add pureed strawberries.
7. Churn again and freeze for another 1 hour.
8. Serve.

Preparation time: 10 minutes
Cooking time: 0 minutes
Total time: 10 minutes
Servings: 2

Nutritional Values

- ➢ *Calories 255*
- ➢ *Total Fat 23.4 g*
- ➢ *Saturated Fat 11.7 g*

- ➤ *Cholesterol 135 mg*
- ➤ *Sodium 112 mg*
- ➤ *Total Carbs 2.5 g*
- ➤ *Sugar 12.5 g*
- ➤ *Fiber 1 g*
- ➤ *Protein 7.9 g*

Mocha Coffee Ice Cream

Ingredients

- ➤ 1 cup of coconut milk
- ➤ ¼ cup heavy whipping cream
- ➤ 2 tablespoons erythritol
- ➤ 2 tablespoons unsweetened cocoa powder
- ➤ 1 tablespoon instant coffee

How to prepare

1. Start by adding everything in a bowl and blend using a handheld blender.
2. Churn this mixture in the ice cream machine as per machine's instructions.
3. Freeze it for 2 hours then garnish with mint and instant coffee.
4. Serve.

Preparation time: 10 minutes

Cooking time: 0 minutes

Total time: 10 minutes

Servings: 2

Nutritional Values

➢ *Calories 259*
➢ *Total Fat 34 g*
➢ *Saturated Fat 10.3 g*
➢ *Cholesterol 112 mg*
➢ *Sodium 92 mg*
➢ *Total Carbs 8.5 g*
➢ *Sugar 2 g*
➢ *Fiber 1.3 g*
➢ *Protein 7.5 g*

Pumpkin-Pecan Ice Cream

Ingredients

- ➢ 1 cup pumpkin puree
- ➢ 2 cups unsweetened coconut milk
- ➢ 3 large egg yolks
- ➢ ½ cup erythritol
- ➢ ½ cup chopped pecans, toasted

How to prepare

1. Start by adding everything in a separate bowl and blend using a hand blender.

2.Churn this mixture in the ice cream machine as per the machine's instructions.

3.Stir in pecans, churn again, then freeze for 4 hours.

4. Enjoy.

Preparation time: 10 minutes

Cooking time: 0 minutes

Total time: 10 minutes

Servings: 4

Nutritional Values

- ➢ *Calories 267*
- ➢ *Total Fat 44.5 g*
- ➢ *Saturated Fat 17.4 g*
- ➢ *Cholesterol 153 mg*
- ➢ *Sodium 217 mg*
- ➢ *Total Carbs 8.4 g*
- ➢ *Sugar 2.3 g*
- ➢ *Fiber 1.3 g*
- ➢ *Protein 3.1 g*

Fresh Raspberry Mousse

Ingredients

- ➤ 2 cups heavy whipping cream
- ➤ 3 ounces fresh raspberries
- ➤ 2 ounces pecans, chopped
- ➤ ½ lemon, the zest
- ➤ ¼ teaspoon vanilla extract

How to prepare

1. Beat cream in a bowl using a hand mixer until it forms peaks.

2. Stir in vanilla and lemon zest, mix well until incorporated.

3. Fold in nuts and berries, mix thoroughly.

4. Cover the berry mixture with plastic wrap and refrigerator for 3 hours.

5. Serve fresh.

Preparation time: 10 minutes

Cooking time: 0 minutes

Total time: 10 minutes

Servings: 4

Nutritional Values

➢ *Calories 331*

➢ *Total Fat 38.5 g*

➢ *Saturated Fat 19.2 g*

➢ *Cholesterol 141 mg*

➢ *Sodium 283 mg*

➢ *Total Carbs 9.2 g*

➢ *Sugar 3 g*

➢ *Fiber 1 g*

➢ *Protein 2.1 g*

Coco Mousse

Ingredients

- ➤ 1 cup heavy whipping cream
- ➤ ¼ cup unsweetened cocoa powder, sifted
- ➤ ¼ cup swerve powdered sweetener
- ➤ 1 teaspoon vanilla extract
- ➤ ¼ teaspoon kosher salt

How to prepare

1. Add cream to the bowl of the electric mixture and beat until it forms peaks.

2. Stir in cocoa powder, vanilla, sweetener, and salt.

3. Mix well until smooth using a hand mixer.

4. Refrigerate for 4 hours.

5. Serve.

Preparation time: 10 minutes

Cooking time: 0 minutes

Total time: 10 minutes

Servings: 4

Nutritional Values

- ➢ *Calories 282*
- ➢ *Total Fat 25.1 g*
- ➢ *Saturated Fat 8.8 g*
- ➢ *Cholesterol 100 mg*
- ➢ *Sodium 117 mg*
- ➢ *Total Carbs 9.4 g*
- ➢ *Sugar 0.7 g*
- ➢ *Fiber 3.2 g*
- ➢ *Protein 8 g*

Peanut Butter Vanilla Mousse

Ingredients

- ½ cup heavy whipping cream
- 4 ounces cream cheese, softened
- ¼ cup natural peanut butter
- ¼ cup powdered swerve sweetener
- ½ teaspoon vanilla extract

How to prepare

1. Beat ½ cup cream in a medium bowl with a hand mixer until it forms peaks.

2. Now beat cream cheese with peanut butter in another bowl until creamy.

3. Stir in vanilla, and sweetener, mix well until smooth.

4. Fold in whipped cream and mix well until fully incorporated.

5. Divide the mouse in the serving glasses.

6. Garnish as desired.

7. Enjoy.

Preparation time: 10 minutes

Cooking time: 0 minutes

Total time: 10 minutes

Servings: 4

Nutritional Values

- ➢ *Calories 214*
- ➢ *Total Fat 19 g*
- ➢ *Saturated Fat 5.8 g*
- ➢ *Cholesterol 15 mg*
- ➢ *Sodium 123 mg*
- ➢ *Total Carbs 6.5 g*
- ➢ *Sugar 1.9 g*
- ➢ *Fiber 2.1 g*
- ➢ *Protein 6.5 g*

Chocolate-Dipped Almond Cookies

Ingredients

- ➤ 1 ½ cups almond flour
- ➤ 1/3 cup almond butter
- ➤ 2 tablespoons powdered erythritol
- ➤ 2 large eggs
- ➤ 3 ounces of 90% dark chocolate

How to prepare

1. Whisk almond flour, baking powder, and erythritol in a mixing bowl.
2. Stir in almond butter and egg to the dry batter
3. Mix well to form a dough then place it in a sandwich bag.
4. Refrigerate for 30 minutes.
5. Let your oven preheat at 285°F.
6. Place the almond dough in between two sheets of parchment then roll it into ½-inch-thick sheet.
7. Use a 2.5-inch diameter cookie cutter to cut the cookies out of this dough.
8. Reroll the remaining dough then place it in the greased baking sheet.
9. Bake the cookies for 30 minutes until golden-brown in color.
10. Place the baked almond cookies on a wire rack to cool down.
11. Melt chocolate in a bowl by heating in a microwave and stir well.
12. Dip half of each almond cookie in the chocolate melt and allow it to set.
13. Refrigerate the dipped cookies for 15 minutes.
14. Serve.

Preparation time: 10 minutes

Cooking time: 30 minutes

Total time: 40 minutes

Servings: 8

Nutritional Values

- ➢ *Calories 266*
- ➢ *Total Fat 25.7 g*
- ➢ *Saturated Fat 1.2 g*
- ➢ *Cholesterol 41 mg*
- ➢ *Sodium 18 mg*
- ➢ *Total Carbs 9.7 g*
- ➢ *Sugar 1.2 g*
- ➢ *Fiber 0.5 g*
- ➢ *Protein 2.6 g*

Keto Pistachio Cookies

Ingredients

- ➤ ¾ cup (4 ounces) shelled pistachio nuts
- ➤ 2 teaspoon, 1 cup stevia granulated sweetener
- ➤ 1 2/3 cup almond flour
- ➤ 2 eggs, beaten well

How to prepare

1. Add pistachio and stevia to a food processor and pulse until finely ground.

2. Toss pistachio mixture with almond meal or flour in a

bowl.

3. Add eggs and whisk well until combined.

4. Refrigerate this mixture for 8 hours or overnight.

5. Let your oven preheat at 325°F.

6. Layer a cookie sheet wax paper then use a scoop to add the cookie dough to the sheet scoop by scoop.

7. Bake them for 25 minutes until lightly brown.

8. Allow them to cool then serve.

Preparation time: 10 minutes

Cooking time: 25 minutes

Total time: 35 minutes

Servings: 8

Nutritional Values

➤ *Calories 174*

➤ *Total Fat 12.3 g*

➤ *Saturated Fat 4.8 g*

➤ *Cholesterol 32 mg*

➤ *Sodium 597 mg*

➤ *Total Carbs 4.5 g*

➤ *Fiber 0.6 g*

➤ *Sugar 1.9 g*

➤ *Protein 12 g*

Strawberry Walnut Cookies

Ingredients

- ➢ 1 cup almond flour
- ➢ 1 large egg, beaten
- ➢ 1/6 cup walnuts, chopped
- ➢ 1/3 cup erythritol
- ➢ 2 ½ tablespoons sugar-free strawberry preserves

How to prepare

1. Start by preheating your oven to 375°F.

2. Beat egg with almond flour and erythritol, in a medium bowl.

3. Make about 1 ½-inch balls out of this mixture and flatten them lightly.

4. Coat cookies with the walnuts then place them on the baking sheet, lined with wax paper.

5. Bake them for 8 minutes then make a small groove at the center of each cookie.

6. Add a teaspoon of jam to the center of each cookie then bake them for 10 minutes.

7. Let them cool down completely.

8. Serve.

Preparation time: 10 minutes

Cooking time: 10 minutes

Total time: 20 minutes

Servings: 8

Nutritional Values

➢ *Calories 101*

➢ *Total Fat 15.5 g*

➢ *Saturated Fat 4.5 g*

➢ *Cholesterol 12 mg*

- *Sodium 18 mg*
- *Total Carbs 4.4 g*
- *Sugar 1.2 g*
- *Fiber 0.3 g*
- *Protein 4.8 g*

Raw Pecan Cookies

Ingredients

- ➤ 1 cup almond flour
- ➤ 1 large egg
- ➤ 4 tablespoons butter, melted
- ➤ ½ cup erythritol
- ➤ 1/3 cup raw pecans, crushed

How to prepare

1. Start by adding all dry ingredients to a bowl then mix

well with a fork.

2. Add egg and mix well until combined

3. Mix this mixture well until fully incorporated.

4. Add pecans to a Ziploc bag and crush them evenly.

5. Transfer these pecans to the cookie dough and mix well.

6. Place the pecans dough on the wax paper and make a rectangular log with your hands.

7. Cover it with more wax paper to freeze for 30 minutes.

8. Meanwhile, preheat your oven for 5 minutes at 350°F.

9. Layer a suitable cookie sheet with wax paper and set it aside.

10. Slice the dough log into ¼-inch-thick slices.

11. Set these slices on the cookie sheet and bake them for 15 minutes.

12. Allow them to cool then serve.

Preparation time: 10 minutes

Cooking time: 20 minutes

Total time: 30 minutes

Servings: 8

Nutritional Values

➢ *Calories 113*

➢ *Total Fat 9 g*

➢ *Saturated Fat 0.2 g*

- ➢ *Cholesterol 1.7 mg*
- ➢ *Sodium 134 mg*
- ➢ *Total Carbs 6.5 g*
- ➢ *Sugar 1.8 g*
- ➢ *Fiber 0.7 g*
- ➢ *Protein 7.5 g*

Part 2: Holiday Christmas Recipes

Chapter 5: Keto Main Dishes Recipes

Garlicky Prime Rib

Ingredients

- 1 (10-pound) prime rib roast
- 10 garlic cloves, minced
- 2 tablespoons olive oil
- 2 teaspoons salt
- 2 teaspoons ground black pepper

How to prepare

1. Mix olive oil with garlic, thyme, black pepper, and salt in a small bowl.
2. Set the prime rib roast in a roasting pan.
3. Rub the garlic mixture over the rib roast.
4. Cover the roast and roast it for 20 minutes in the preheated oven.
5. Now lower the temperature to 325°F and roast for 60–75 minutes until the internal temperature of the beef roast reaches 135°F.
6. Leave the roast for 15 minutes at room temperature.
7. Slice and serve warm.

Preparation time: 10 minutes

Cooking time: 1 hour 45 minutes

Total time: 1 hour 55 minutes

Servings: 10

Nutritional Values

- ➤ *Calories 311*
- ➤ *Total Fat 24.9 g*
- ➤ *Saturated Fat 3.5 g*
- ➤ *Cholesterol 3 mg*
- ➤ *Sodium 243 mg*
- ➤ *Total Carbohydrates 1.8 g*
- ➤ *Dietary Fiber 3.3 g*
- ➤ *Sugars 11.9 g*
- ➤ *Protein 47.1 g*

Egg Sausage Casserole

Ingredients

- ➢ 12 large eggs, beaten
- ➢ 2 pounds ground sausage
- ➢ 16 ounces shredded cheddar cheese

How to Prepare

1. Set a large iron skillet over medium-high heat.

2. Add breakfast sausage and sauté until brown.

3. Beat all the 12 eggs in a large glass bowl and pour it into a

9x13-inch greased baking dish.

4. Stir in breakfast sausage and drizzle cheese on top.

5. Cover the dish with a foil sheet and bake for 15 minutes at 350°F.

6. Uncover and garnish as desired.

7. Slice and serve.

Preparation time: 10 minutes

Cooking time: 15 minutes

Total time: 25 minutes

Servings: 8

Nutritional Values

➢ *Calories 261*

➢ *Total Fat 27.1 g*

➢ *Saturated Fat 23.4 g*

➢ *Cholesterol 0 mg*

➢ *Sodium 10 mg*

➢ *Total Carbs 6.1 g*

➢ *Sugar 2.1 g*

➢ *Fiber 3.9 g*

➢ *Protein 1.8 g*

Easy Salmon Patties

Ingredients

- ➢ 1 (14.75-ounce) can canned salmon
- ➢ 1 egg
- ➢ ½ cup almond flour
- ➢ 1-quart vegetable oil for frying

How to Prepare

1. Mix salmon with egg and almond flour in a mixing bowl.
2. Make 4 patties out of the salmon mixture.

3. Set a suitable fry pan over medium-high heat and heat oil for frying.

4. Place the patties in the oil and cook until golden-brown.

5. Drain and transfer the patties to a plate.

6. Serve warm.

Preparation time: 10 minutes

Cooking time: 0 minutes

Total time: 10 minutes

Servings: 4

Nutritional Values

- ➤ *Calories 139*
- ➤ *Total Fat 4.6 g*
- ➤ *Saturated Fat 0.5 g*
- ➤ *Cholesterol 1.2 mg*
- ➤ *Sodium 83 mg*
- ➤ *Total Carbs 7.5 g*
- ➤ *Sugar 6.3 g*
- ➤ *Fiber 0.6 g*
- ➤ *Protein 23.8 g*

Lamb Leg Roast

Ingredients

- ➢ 4 garlic cloves, sliced
- ➢ 2 tablespoons fresh rosemary
- ➢ Salt, to taste
- ➢ Ground black pepper, to taste
- ➢ 5 pounds leg of lamb

How to Prepare

1. Set the oven for preheating at 350°F.

2. Place the lamb leg in a roasting pan and rub it generously with salt and black pepper.

3. Place the sliced garlic and rosemary on top of the lamb.

4. Roast the lamb leg for 2 hours in the preheated oven.

5. Leave the roasted leg for 10 minutes at room temperature.

6. Serve warm.

Preparation time: 10 minutes

Cooking time: 2 hours

Total time: 2 hours 10 minutes

Servings: 8

Nutritional Values

➢ Calories 350

➢ Total Fat 21.1 g

➢ Saturated Fat 19.5 g

➢ Cholesterol 14.2 mg

➢ Sodium 46 mg

➢ Total Carbs 1.1 g

➢ Sugar 1.3 g

➢ Fiber 0.4 g

➢ Protein 40.4 g

Herb-Butter Chicken Roast

Ingredients

- ➢ 4 pounds whole chicken, giblets and neck removed
- ➢ ¼ cup unsalted butter, melted
- ➢ 3 tablespoons olive oil
- ➢ ¼ cup white wine
- ➢ 1 lemon, halved
- ➢ Salt and freshly ground pepper, to taste
- ➢ 2 tablespoons fresh parsley, chopped

- ➢ 4 garlic cloves, minced
- ➢ 1 head of garlic, peeled and sliced
- ➢ 3 fresh whole rosemary sprigs

How to Prepare

1. Set the oven for preheating at 430°F.
2. Layer a roasting pan with a foil sheet and place the chicken in it.
3. Mix butter, wine, melted butter, oil, and lemon juice in a bowl.
4. Pour this mixture over the chicken and inside its cavity.
5. Rub the chicken with salt, garlic, and black pepper.
6. Mix and spread all the remaining ingredients around the chicken.
7. Roast it for 1 hour 15 minutes in the preheated oven.
8. Serve warm.

Preparation time: 10 minutes
Cooking time: 1 hour 20 minutes
Total time: 1 hour 30 minutes
Servings: 8

Nutritional Values

- ➢ *Calories 336*
- ➢ *Total Fat 10.7 g*

- *Saturated Fat 0.5 g*
- *Cholesterol 4 mg*
- *Sodium 45 mg*
- *Total Carbs 1.2 g*
- *Sugar 1.4 g*
- *Fiber 0 g*
- *Protein 43 g*

Chicken Skewers

Ingredients

- ¼ cup vegetable oil
- 1/3 cup choc zero maple syrup
- 1/3 cup soy sauce
- ¼ teaspoon ground black pepper
- 8 skinless, boneless chicken breasts, cubed
- 2 garlic cloves
- 5 small onions, diced into 2-inch pieces
- 2 red bell peppers, diced into 2-inch pieces

How to Prepare

1. Set the grill temperature to medium and grease its grilling grates with cooking oil.
2. Mix maple syrup, soy sauce, oil, garlic, and black pepper in a small bowl.
3. Add onions, red bell pepper, and chicken cubes to a large bowl.
4. Pour the maple mixture into this bowl and toss well.
5. Thread the chicken cubes with bell pepper and onion on the skewers, alternately.
6. Grill each skewer for 3 minutes per side until golden-brown.
7. Serve warm.

Preparation time: 10 minutes
Cooking time: 20 minutes
Total time: 30 minutes
Servings: 8

Nutritional Values

➢ *Calories 321*
➢ *Total Fat 4.7 g*
➢ *Saturated Fat 0.8 g*
➢ *Cholesterol 11 mg*
➢ *Sodium 43 mg*

- ➤ *Total Carbs 0 g*
- ➤ *Sugar 0.2 g*
- ➤ *Fiber 0.5 g*
- ➤ *Protein 42 g*

Christmas Goose

Ingredients

- ➢ 1 whole smoked goose
- ➢ 3 cups water
- ➢ ½ cup red wine
- ➢ ¼ cup aged balsamic vinegar
- ➢ 1 cup blackberries
- ➢ ½ teaspoon ground black pepper
- ➢ Salt, to taste

➤ 2 tablespoons butter

How to Prepare

1. Set the oven for preheating at 350°F.

2. Thoroughly clean the goose inside out and place it in a roasting pan.

3. Drizzle butter, salt, and black pepper on top.

4. Roast this goose for 1 hour 15 minutes in the preheated oven.

5. Meanwhile, mix blackberries with red wine and vinegar in a saucepan.

6. Cook this glaze on a simmer until it is thick and bubbly.

7. Once the goose is roasted, pour the glaze on top.

8. Serve warm.

Preparation time: 10 minutes

Cooking time: 1 hour 25 minutes

Total time: 1 hour 35 minutes

Servings: 4

Nutritional Values

➤ *Calories 438*
➤ *Total Fat 0.6 g*
➤ *Saturated Fat 0 g*
➤ *Cholesterol 0 mg*

- *Sodium 33 mg*
- *Total Carbs 2.4 g*
- *Sugar 0 g*
- *Fiber 0 g*
- *Protein 56 g*

5-Spice Roasted Duck

Ingredients

- ➤ 1 (5-pound) duck, necks and giblets removed
- ➤ 3 tablespoons salt
- ➤ 1 tablespoon Chinese 5-spice powder
- ➤ 1 tablespoon garlic powder

How to Prepare

1. Set the oven for preheating at 350°F.
2. Thoroughly clean the duck from inside out and score its

138

skin with a paring knife.

3. Mix salt with 5-spice powder and garlic powder in a small.

4. Place the cleaned duck in a roasting pan and rub it with spice mixture from all the sides.

5. Roast this duck for 2 hours in the preheated oven.

6. Flip the duck every 30 minutes.

7. Serve warm.

Preparation time: 10 minutes
Cooking time: 2 hours
Total time: 2 hours 10 minutes
Servings: 8

Nutritional Values

- ➤ *Calories 376*
- ➤ *Total Fat 7.2 g*
- ➤ *Saturated Fat 6.4 g*
- ➤ *Cholesterol 0 mg*
- ➤ *Sodium 8 mg*
- ➤ *Total Carbs 2g*
- ➤ *Sugar 1 g*
- ➤ *Fiber 0.7 g*
- ➤ *Protein 42.2 g*

Salmon Pecan Bake

Ingredients

- ➤ 3 tablespoons Dijon mustard
- ➤ 4 tablespoons butter, melted
- ➤ ½ cup almond meal
- ➤ ½ cup pecans, chopped
- ➤ 3 teaspoons fresh parsley, chopped
- ➤ 6 (4-ounce) fillets salmon
- ➤ Salt and black pepper, to taste
- ➤ 6 wedge lemon wedges

How to Prepare

1. Set the oven for preheating at 400°F.
2. Mix mustard with melted butter in one bowl and mix pecans with almond meal and parsley in another bowl.
3. Place the cleaned salmon fillets in a baking pan and rub them with salt and black pepper.
4. Brush the butter mustard mixture over the fillets then pour the rest on top.
5. Drizzle the pecans mixture over the salmon.
6. Bake these fillets for 10 minutes in the preheated oven.
7. Garnish with lemon wedges.
8. Serve warm.

Preparation time: 10 minutes

Cooking time: 10 minutes

Total time: 20 minutes

Servings: 6

Nutritional Values

➤ *Calories 293*
➤ *Total Fat 20 g*
➤ *Saturated Fat 13.2 g*
➤ *Cholesterol 10 mg*
➤ *Sodium 8 mg*
➤ *Total Carbs 2.5 g*

- Sugar 1 g
- Fiber 0.7 g
- Protein 34.2 g

Mushroom-Stuffed Cornish Hens

Ingredients

- ½ cup melted butter
- ½ onion, chopped
- ½ stalk celery, chopped
- ¼ green bell pepper, chopped
- 2 whole birds Cornish game hens
- 1 (4.5-ounce) can mushrooms, diced and drained

- ➤ 2 garlic cloves, minced
- ➤ 1 tablespoon dried basil
- ➤ 1 teaspoon dried oregano
- ➤ 1 tablespoon fresh parsley, chopped
- ➤ ¼ cup butter, melted

How to prepare

1. Set the oven for preheating at 325ºF.
2. Mix ½ cup melted butter with celery, mushrooms, garlic, basil, parsley, oregano, bell pepper, and onion in a suitable bowl.
3. Mix the remaining butter with basil, oregano, and parsley in a small bowl.
4. Place the hens in the roasting pan and rub them with the butter herbs mixture.
5. Stuff each hen with half of the mushroom stuffing.
6. Cover the roasting pans and roast each hen for 1 ½ hour in the preheated oven.
7. Remove the cover and continue roasting at 500ºF until the hens turn golden-brown from top.
8. Serve warm.

Preparation time: 10 minutes
Cooking time: 1 hour 30 minutes
Total time: 1 hour 40 minutes
Servings: 12

Nutritional Values

- Calories 451
- Total Fat 23.9 g
- Saturated Fat 2.1 g
- Cholesterol 0 mg
- Sodium 2,574 mg
- Total Carbohydrates 6.7 g
- Dietary Fiber 4.5 g
- Sugars 1.1 g
- Protein 56.7 g

Chapter 6: Keto Meat and Poultry Recipes

Creamy Beef Bake

Ingredients

- 12 ounces cauliflower rice
- 1 ½ pounds lean ground beef
- 15 ounces sugar-free tomato sauce
- ½ cup sour cream

- ➢ 3 cups cheddar cheese, shredded
- ➢ Salt and black pepper, to taste

How to prepare

1. Start by sautéing cauliflower rice in a non-stick skillet over medium heat for 5 minutes.
2. Toss in ground beef and stir cook until it is brown.
3. Add tomato sauce, sour cream, and cheese.
4. Mix well then bake the mixture for 15 minutes at 300°F.
5. Serve fresh and warm.

Preparation time: 10 minutes
Cooking time: 20 minutes
Total time: 25 minutes
Servings: 6

Nutritional Values

- ➢ *Calories 327*
- ➢ *Total Fat 16.6 g*
- ➢ *Saturated Fat 2.1 g*
- ➢ *Cholesterol 20 mg*
- ➢ *Sodium 292 mg*
- ➢ *Total Carbs 2.3 g*
- ➢ *Fiber 1.7 g*
- ➢ *Sugar 0.2 g*
- ➢ *Protein 13.8 g*

Beef Taco Fry

Ingredients

- ➢ 1 pound ground beef
- ➢ ½ white onion, diced
- ➢ 3 tablespoons taco seasoning
- ➢ 2 Roma tomatoes, seeded and diced
- ➢ 12 ounces cauliflower rice

How to prepare

1. Start by adding beef to a suitable skillet.
2. Stir cook for 5 minutes then adds onion and taco seasoning.
3. Sauté for 3 minutes, then tomatoes and cauliflower rice.
4. Continue cooking for approximately 7 minutes.
5. Serve fresh and warm.

Preparation time: 10 minutes

Cooking time: 17 minutes

Total time: 27 minutes

Servings: 4

Nutritional Values

➢ *Calories 301*
➢ *Total Fat 12.2 g*
➢ *Saturated Fat 2.4 g*
➢ *Cholesterol 110 mg*
➢ *Sodium 276 mg*
➢ *Total Carbs 2.4 g*
➢ *Fiber 0.9 g*
➢ *Sugar 1.4 g*
➢ *Protein 28.8 g*

Philly Beef Casserole

Ingredients

- ➢ 1 ½ pounds lean ground beef
- ➢ 1 garlic clove
- ➢ 4 slices Provolone cheese
- ➢ 4 large eggs
- ➢ ½ cup heavy cream
- ➢ Salt and black pepper, to taste

How to prepare

1. Start by adding beef to a suitable non-stick skillet.

2. Add salt, pepper, and garlic, sauté until beef turns brown.

3. Whisk eggs with cream in a separate bowl.

4. First, spread the beef in a casserole dish.

5. Pour the egg-cream mixture over the beef evenly then top it with cheese slices.

6. Bake the beef casserole at 350°F for 35 minutes.

7. Slice and serve fresh.

Preparation time: 10 minutes

Cooking time: 35 minutes

Total time: 45 minutes

Servings: 8

Nutritional Values

➢ *Calories 421*

➢ *Total Fat 12.2 g*

➢ *Saturated Fat 2.4 g*

➢ *Cholesterol 110 mg*

➢ *Sodium 276 mg*

➢ *Total Carbs 7.5 g*

➢ *Fiber 0.9 g*

➢ *Sugar 1.4 g*

➢ *Protein 18.8 g*

Cauliflower Beef Soup

Ingredients

- ➢ 1 pound ground beef
- ➢ 1 head cauliflower, chopped
- ➢ 3 ½ cups chicken broth
- ➢ 1 cup unsweetened almond milk
- ➢ ½ cup heavy cream
- ➢ Salt and black pepper, to taste

How to prepare

1. Start by adding ground beef to a suitable skillet.

2. Sauté for 10 minutes until al dente and brown.

3. Add almond milk, broth, cauliflower, salt, and black pepper.

4. Cook on a boil then let it simmer for 15 minutes until cauliflower is cooked.

5. Serve warm and fresh with desired garnishes.

Preparation time: 10 minutes
Cooking time: 25 minutes
Total time: 35 minutes
Servings: 6

Nutritional Values

- ➤ *Calories 272*
- ➤ *Total Fat 18 g*
- ➤ *Saturated Fat 5 g*
- ➤ *Cholesterol 6.1 mg*
- ➤ *Sodium 3 mg*
- ➤ *Total Carbs 4 g*
- ➤ *Fiber 3 g*
- ➤ *Sugar 4 g*
- ➤ *Protein 19.4 g*

Beef with Sriracha Coleslaw

Ingredients

- ➤ 2 garlic cloves
- ➤ 2 tablespoons sesame seed oil
- ➤ 1 pound ground beef
- ➤ 10 ounces coleslaw salad mix
- ➤ 1 tablespoon sriracha
- ➤ Salt and black pepper, to taste

How to prepare

1. Start by heating the oil in a suitable pan.

2. Add garlic and sauté for 30 seconds, then add beef.

3. Stir cook for 10 minutes until it is brown.

4. Add Coleslaw salad mixture.

5. Mix well then add sriracha, stir for 5 minutes.

6. Adjust seasoning with salt and black pepper.

7. Garnish as desired, then serve fresh and warm.

Preparation time: 10 minutes

Cooking time: 16 minutes

Total time: 26 minutes

Servings: 4

Nutritional Values

➢ *Calories 388*

➢ *Total Fat 6 g*

➢ *Saturated Fat 1 g*

➢ *Cholesterol 72 mg*

➢ *Sodium 472 mg*

➢ *Total Carbs 5 g*

➢ *Fiber 1.6 g*

➢ *Sugar 2.3 g*

➢ *Protein 22.5 g*

Thyme-Rubbed Rotisserie Chicken

Ingredients

- ➤ 1 organic whole chicken
- ➤ 1 tablespoon olive oil
- ➤ 1 teaspoon thyme
- ➤ 1 teaspoon rosemary
- ➤ 1 teaspoon garlic, granulated

➢ Salt and black pepper

How to prepare

1. Start by seasoning the chicken with all the herbs and spices.
2. Broil this seasoned chicken for 5 minutes in the oven until golden-brown.
3. Place this chicken in the Crockpot.
4. Cover it and cook for 8 hours on low setting.
5. Serve warm.

Preparation time: 10 minutes
Cooking time: 8hours 5 minutes
Total time: 8 hours 15 minutes
Servings: 8

Nutritional Values

➢ *Calories 301*
➢ *Total Fat 12.2 g*
➢ *Saturated Fat 2.4 g*
➢ *Cholesterol 110 mg*
➢ *Total Carbs 2.5 g*
➢ *Fiber 0.9 g*
➢ *Sugar 1.4 g*
➢ *Sodium 276 mg*
➢ *Protein 28.8 g*

Adobo Chicken Drumsticks

Ingredients

- ¼ cup apple cider vinegar
- 12 chicken drumsticks
- 1 onion, chopped into slices
- 2 tablespoons olive oil
- 10 garlic cloves, smashed
- 1 cup gluten-free tamari
- ¼ cup green onion, chopped

How to prepare

1. Place the drumsticks in the Crockpot and then add the remaining ingredients on top.

2. Cover it and cook for 8 hours on low setting.

3. Mix gently, then serve warm.

Preparation time: 10 minutes

Cooking time: 8 hours

Total time: 8 hours 10 minutes

Servings: 12

Nutritional Values

➤ *Calories 249*

➤ *Total Fat 11.9 g*

➤ *Saturated Fat 1.7 g*

➤ *Cholesterol 78 mg*

➤ *Total Carbs 1.8 g*

➤ *Fiber 1.1 g*

➤ *Sugar 0.3 g*

➤ *Sodium 79 mg*

➤ *Protein 25 g*

Ginger Chicken

Ingredients

- ➢ 1 ½ pounds chicken drumsticks, skin removed
- ➢ 1 (13.5-ounce) can coconut milk
- ➢ 1 onion, chopped
- ➢ 4 garlic cloves, minced
- ➢ 1-inch knob fresh ginger, minced
- ➢ 1 Serrano pepper, minced
- ➢ 1 tablespoon Garam Masala

- ½ teaspoon cayenne
- ½ teaspoon paprika
- ½ teaspoon turmeric
- Salt and black pepper, to taste

How to prepare

1. Start by throwing all the ingredients into the Crockpot.

2. Cover it and cook for 6 hours on low setting.

3. Garnish as desired.

4. Serve warm.

Preparation time: 10 minutes

Cooking time: 6 hours

Total time: 6 hours 10 minutes

Servings: 4

Nutritional Values

- *Calories 248*
- *Total Fat 15.7 g*
- *Saturated Fat 2.7 g*
- *Cholesterol 75 mg*
- *Total Carbs 8.4 g*
- *Fiber 0g*
- *Sugar 1.1 g*
- *Sodium 94 mg*
- *Protein 14.1 g*

Easy Chicken Stew

Ingredients

- ➤ 1 can coconut milk
- ➤ ½ cup chicken stock
- ➤ 1 pound boneless, skinless chicken thighs, diced
- ➤ 1 2 tablespoons red curry paste
- ➤ 1 tablespoon coconut aminos
- ➤ 1 tablespoon fish sauce

- ➢ 3 garlic cloves, minced
- ➢ Salt and pepper, to taste
- ➢ Red pepper flakes, as desired
- ➢ 1 bag frozen mixed vegetables

How to prepare

1. Start by throwing all the ingredients (except vegetables) into the Crockpot.
2. Cover it and cook for 2 hours on low setting.
3. Remove its lid and thawed vegetables.
4. Cover the crockpot again then continue cooking for another 30 minutes on low setting.
5. Garnish as desired.
6. Serve warm.

Preparation time: 10 minutes

Cooking time: 2 hours

Total time: 2 hours 10 minutes

Servings: 4

Nutritional Values

- ➢ *Calories 327*
- ➢ *Total Fat 3.5 g*
- ➢ *Saturated Fat 0.5 g*
- ➢ *Cholesterol 162 mg*

- *Total Carbs 56 g*
- *Fiber 0.4 g*
- *Sugar 0.5 g*
- *Sodium 142 mg*
- *Protein 21.5 g*

Lemongrass Chicken Drumsticks

Ingredients

- ➢ 10 drumsticks, skin removed
- ➢ 1 thick stalk fresh lemongrass
- ➢ 4 garlic cloves, minced
- ➢ 1 thumb-size piece of ginger
- ➢ 1 cup of coconut milk
- ➢ 2 tablespoons Red Boat fish sauce
- ➢ 3 tablespoons coconut aminos

- 1 teaspoon five-spice powder
- 1 large onion, thinly sliced
- ¼ cup fresh scallions, chopped
- Kosher salt
- Freshly ground black pepper

How to prepare

1. Start by throwing all the ingredients into the Crockpot.
2. Cover it and cook for 5 hours on low setting.
3. Garnish as desired.
4. Serve warm.

Preparation time: 10 minutes
Cooking time: 5 hours
Total time: 5 hours 10 minutes
Servings: 10

Nutritional Values

- *Calories 372*
- *Total Fat 11.1 g*
- *Saturated Fat 5.8 g*
- *Cholesterol 610 mg*
- *Total Carbs 0.9 g*
- *Fiber 0.2 g*
- *Sugar 0.2 g*
- *Sodium 749 mg*
- *Protein 63.5 g*

Chapter 7: Keto Salad Recipes

Kale Tahini Salad

Ingredients

Dressing

➢ 2 limes juiced

- Zest of 1 lime
- 2 tablespoons fish sauce
- 2 tablespoons ponzu sauce
- 2–3 tablespoons sweet Thai chili sauce
- 1–2 garlic cloves minced or grated
- 1 tablespoon fresh ginger grated
- 2–3 tablespoons tahini

Salad

- 3–4 cups baby kale or other dark leafy greens
- 1 (1-ounce) bag frozen shelled edamame, defrosted and cooked
- 3 carrots, shredded
- 2 bell peppers (red, yellow, or orange), thinly sliced
- 2 lemongrass stalks, chopped
- 4 green onions, chopped
- ¾ cup of fresh basil and cilantro
- 4 hard-boiled eggs, diced
- ¼ cup black and/or white sesame seeds, toasted

How to prepare

1. Mix all the ingredients for tahini dressing in a salad bowl.
2. Toss in the remaining ingredients and mix gently.
3. Enjoy.

Preparation time: 10 minutes

Cooking time: 0 minutes

Total time: 10 minutes

Servings: 8

Nutritional Values

- ➤ *Calories 132*
- ➤ *Total Fat 6.9 g*
- ➤ *Saturated Fat 1.4 g*
- ➤ *Cholesterol 93 mg*
- ➤ *Sodium 405 mg*
- ➤ *Total Carbohydrates 10.4 g*
- ➤ *Dietary Fiber 3.1 g*
- ➤ *Sugars 5.6 g*
- ➤ *Protein 6.4 g*

Chicken Salad

Ingredients

- ➤ ½ cup almond butter, melted
- ➤ 1 cooked chicken breast, shredded
- ➤ 1 tablespoon soy sauce
- ➤ 1 teaspoon sesame oil
- ➤ 4 tablespoons water
- ➤ 1 cucumber, peeled and sliced
- ➤ 1 tablespoon sambal oelek
- ➤ 2 tablespoons peanuts, chopped

How to prepare

1. Whisk and mix all the ingredients for dressing in a salad bowl.
2. Toss in the remaining ingredients and mix gently.
3. Enjoy.

Preparation time: 10 minutes

Cooking time: 0 minutes

Total time: 10 minutes

Servings: 2

Nutritional Values

- ➤ *Calories 179*
- ➤ *Total Fat 10.4 g*
- ➤ *Saturated Fat 1.2 g*
- ➤ *Cholesterol 32 mg*
- ➤ *Sodium 520 mg*
- ➤ *Total Carbohydrates 8.4 g*
- ➤ *Dietary Fiber 2 g*
- ➤ *Sugars 3.7 g*
- ➤ *Protein 15.3 g*

Spinach Cranberry Salad

Ingredients

- ➤ 1 tablespoon almond butter, melted
- ➤ ¾ cup almonds, blanched
- ➤ 1 pound spinach, rinsed and torn into pieces
- ➤ 1 cup dried cranberries
- ➤ 2 tablespoons toasted sesame seeds
- ➤ 1 tablespoon poppy seeds
- ➤ ½ cup Swerve
- ➤ 2 teaspoons onion, minced
- ➤ ¼ teaspoon paprika

- ¼ cup white wine vinegar
- ¼ cup cider vinegar
- ½ cup vegetable oil

How to prepare

1. Mix all the ingredients for cranberry salad in a salad bowl.
2. Enjoy.

Preparation time: 10 minutes
Cooking time: 0 minutes
Total time: 10 minutes
Servings: 6

Nutritional Values

- *Calories 141*
- *Total Fat 9.9 g*
- *Saturated Fat 0.9 g*
- *Cholesterol 0 mg*
- *Sodium 61 mg*
- *Total Carbohydrates 8.9 g*
- *Dietary Fiber 4.6 g*
- *Sugars 1.9 g*
- *Protein 6.1 g*

Broccoli Mayo Salad

Ingredients

- ➤ 10 slices bacon
- ➤ 1 head fresh broccoli, cut into pieces
- ➤ ¼ cup red onion, chopped
- ➤ 3 tablespoons white wine vinegar
- ➤ 2 tablespoons swerve
- ➤ 1 cup mayonnaise
- ➤ 1 cup sunflower seeds

How to prepare

1. Sauté bacon in a deep skillet for 5 minutes until crispy.

2. Drain the bacon and crumble it. Set it aside.

3. Mix all the ingredients for mayo salad in a salad bowl.

4. Enjoy.

Preparation time: 10 minutes

Cooking time: 5 minutes

Total time: 15 minutes

Servings: 6

Nutritional Values

- *Calories 235*
- *Total Fat 17.2 g*
- *Saturated Fat 4.7 g*
- *Cholesterol 35 mg*
- *Sodium 751 mg*
- *Total Carbohydrates 4.4 g*
- *Dietary Fiber 1.2 g*
- *Sugars 0.7 g*
- *Protein 13.8 g*

Sweet Cucumber Salad

Ingredients

- ➢ 4 cucumbers, thinly sliced
- ➢ 1 small white onion, thinly sliced
- ➢ 1 cup white vinegar
- ➢ ½ cup water
- ➢ ¾ cup Swerve
- ➢ 1 tablespoon dried dill, or to taste

How to prepare

1. Mix all the ingredients for cucumber salad in a salad bowl.
2. Enjoy.

Preparation time: 10 minutes

Cooking time: 0 minutes

Total time: 10 minutes

Servings: 4

Nutritional Values

- *Calories 6*
- *Total Fat 0.4 g*
- *Saturated Fat 0.1 g*
- *Cholesterol 0 mg*
- *Sodium 11 mg*
- *Total Carbohydrates 11.5 g*
- *Dietary Fiber 1.9 g*
- *Sugars 6 g*
- *Protein 2.2 g*

Cucumber Jalapeno Salad

Ingredients

- ➤ 3 large English cucumbers, peeled and cut into slices
- ➤ 1 tablespoon salt
- ➤ ½ cup Swerve
- ➤ ½ cup rice wine vinegar
- ➤ 2 jalapeno peppers, seeded and chopped
- ➤ ¼ cup chopped cilantro
- ➤ ½ cup chopped peanuts

How to prepare

1. Place the cucumber in a suitable colander and sprinkle salt over it.
2. Leave the cucumber for 30 minutes then drain it.
3. Mix all the ingredients for this salad in a salad bowl.
4. Enjoy.

Preparation time: 10 minutes
Cooking time: 0 minutes
Total time: 10 minutes
Servings: 6

Nutritional Values

- *Calories 107*
- *Total Fat 6.2 g*
- *Saturated Fat 0.9 g*
- *Cholesterol 0 mg*
- *Sodium 1,291 mg*
- *Total Carbohydrates 8 g*
- *Dietary Fiber 2 g*
- *Sugars 3.2 g*
- *Protein 4.2 g*

Greens Cranberry Salad

Ingredients

- ➢ 1 cup almonds, sliced
- ➢ 3 tablespoons red wine vinegar
- ➢ 1/3 cup olive oil
- ➢ ¼ cup fresh cranberries
- ➢ 1 tablespoon Dijon mustard
- ➢ ½ teaspoon minced garlic
- ➢ ½ teaspoon salt
- ➢ ½ teaspoon ground black pepper

- ➢ 2 tablespoons water
- ➢ ½ red onion, thinly sliced
- ➢ 1 pound mixed salad greens

How to prepare

1. Let your oven preheat at 375°F.
2. Spread almonds on a baking sheet and roast them for 5 minutes in the oven.
3. Toss the almonds with greens and onion in a salad bowl.
4. Blend the remaining ingredients then pour it into the salad bowl.
5. Toss them well together.
6. Serve fresh.

Preparation time: 10 minutes

Cooking time: 5 minutes

Total time: 15 minutes

Servings: 6

Nutritional Values

- ➢ *Calories 210*
- ➢ *Total Fat 19.3 g*
- ➢ *Saturated Fat 2.2 g*
- ➢ *Cholesterol 0 mg*
- ➢ *Sodium 244 mg*

- *Total Carbohydrates 7.5 g*
- *Dietary Fiber 2.5 g*
- *Sugars 1.3 g*
- *Protein 4.5 g*

Spinach Almond Salad

Ingredients

- ➢ 8 cups baby spinach leaves
- ➢ ½ medium red onion, sliced and rings separated
- ➢ 1 ½ cups sweetened dried cranberries
- ➢ 1 cup almonds, toasted and sliced
- ➢ 1 cup balsamic vinaigrette salad dressing

How to prepare

1. Mix all the ingredients for spinach salad in a salad bowl.

2. Enjoy.

Preparation time: 10 minutes

Cooking time: 0 minutes

Total time: 10 minutes

Servings: 8

Nutritional Values

- ➢ *Calories 215*
- ➢ *Total Fat 12.5 g*
- ➢ *Saturated Fat 6.8 g*
- ➢ *Cholesterol 58 mg*
- ➢ *Sodium 130 mg*
- ➢ *Total Carbohydrates 1.9 g*
- ➢ *Dietary Fiber 0.1 g*
- ➢ *Sugars 1.8 g*
- ➢ *Protein 3.9 g*

Cucumber Ginger Salad

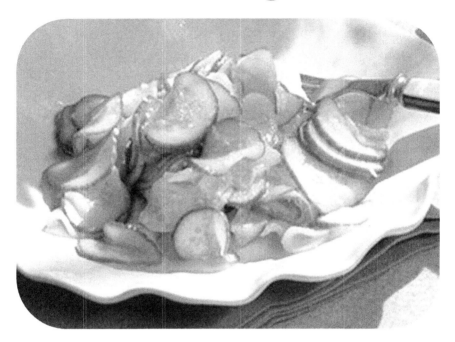

Ingredients

- ➢ 2 large cucumbers; peeled, seeds removed, sliced
- ➢ 1/3 cup rice vinegar
- ➢ 4 teaspoons swerve
- ➢ 1 teaspoon salt
- ➢ 1 ½ teaspoons ginger root, minced

How to prepare

1. Mix all the ingredients for cucumber ginger salad in a salad bowl.

2. Enjoy.

Preparation time: 10 minutes

Cooking time: 0 minutes

Total time: 10 minutes

Servings: 2

Nutritional Values

- ➢ *Calories 83*
- ➢ *Total Fat 0.4 g*
- ➢ *Saturated Fat 0.1 g*
- ➢ *Cholesterol 0 mg*
- ➢ *Sodium 1,169 mg*
- ➢ *Total Carbohydrates 1.1 g*
- ➢ *Dietary Fiber 1.5 g*
- ➢ *Total Sugars 5.1 g*
- ➢ *Protein 2 g*

Strawberry Spinach Salad

Ingredients

- 2 tablespoons sesame seeds
- 1 tablespoon poppy seeds
- ½ cup Swerve
- ½ cup olive oil
- ¼ cup distilled white vinegar
- ¼ teaspoon paprika
- ¼ teaspoon Worcestershire sauce
- 1 tablespoon onion, minced

- 10 ounces fresh spinach; rinsed, dried, torn
- 1 quart strawberries; cleaned, hulled, sliced
- ¼ cup almonds, blanched and slivered

How to prepare

1. Mix all the ingredients for strawberry spinach salad in a salad bowl.

2. Enjoy.

Preparation time: 10 minutes
Cooking time: 0 minutes
Total time: 10 minutes
Servings: 6

Nutritional Values

- *Calories 237*
- *Total Fat 21.4 g*
- *Saturated Fat 2.9 g*
- *Cholesterol 0 mg*
- *Sodium 42 mg*
- *Total Carbohydrates 11.5 g*
- *Dietary Fiber 4 g*
- *Total Sugars 5.4 g*
- *Protein 3.7 g*

Chapter 8: Side Dish Recipes

Savory French Green Beans

Ingredients

- 16 cups frozen French-style green beans, thawed
- ½ cup butter, melted
- ½ cup packed brown Swerve

- 1 ½ teaspoons garlic salt
- ¾ teaspoon reduced-sodium soy sauce

How to prepare

1. Sauté green beans with butter in a suitable skillet for 1 minute.
2. Stir in brown swerve, garlic salt, and soy sauce.
3. Continue sautéing for 5 minutes on medium heat.
4. Serve warm.

Preparation time: 10 minutes
Cooking time: 10 minutes
Total time: 20 minutes
Servings: 9

Nutritional Values

- *Calories 237*
- *Total Fat 22 g*
- *Saturated Fat 9 g*
- *Cholesterol 35 mg*
- *Sodium 118 mg*
- *Total Carbs 5 g*
- *Sugar 1 g*
- *Fiber 2 g*
- *Protein 5 g*

Smoked Party Sausages

Ingredients

- ➢ 2 pounds smoked sausage links, sliced
- ➢ 1 (8-ounce) bottle Catalina salad dressing
- ➢ 1 (8-ounce) bottle Russian salad dressing
- ➢ ½ cup packed brown Swerve
- ➢ ½ cup apple cider
- ➢ Sliced green onions, optional

How to prepare

1. Add sausage slices to a suitable skillet and place it over medium heat.

2. Stir in salad dressing, brown Swerve, and apple cider.

3. Toss and cook for 7 minutes, then garnish with green onions.

4. Serve warm.

Preparation time: 10 minutes

Cooking time: 7 minutes

Total time: 17 minutes

Servings: 8

Nutritional Values

➢ *Calories 190*

➢ *Total Fat 17.25 g*

➢ *Saturated Fat 7.1 g*

➢ *Cholesterol 20 mg*

➢ *Total Carbs 5.5 g*

➢ *Sugar 2.8 g*

➢ *Fiber 3.8 g*

➢ *Sodium 28 mg*

➢ *Protein 23 g*

Collard Ham Mix

Ingredients

- ➢ 4 bunches collard greens, trimmed and chopped
- ➢ 1 pound ham shanks, chopped
- ➢ 4 pickled jalapeno peppers, chopped
- ➢ 1 teaspoon olive oil
- ➢ Ground black pepper, to taste
- ➢ Garlic powder, to taste
- ➢ ¼ cup vegetable stock

How to prepare

1. Set a suitable skillet over medium heat and add olive oil.

2. Stir in ham shanks, collard greens, jalapeno peppers, black pepper, garlic powder.

3. Mix well and sauté for 5 minutes.

4. Pour in vegetable stock and cook the mixture for 5 minutes on a simmer.

5. Serve warm.

Preparation time: 10 minutes

Cooking time: 10 minutes

Total time: 20 minutes

Servings: 6

Nutritional Values

➢ *Calories 121*

➢ *Total Fat 12.9 g*

➢ *Saturated Fat 5.1 g*

➢ *Cholesterol 17 mg*

➢ *Total Carbs 8.1 g*

➢ *Sugar 1.8 g*

➢ *Fiber 0.4 g*

➢ *Sodium 28 mg*

➢ *Protein 5.4 g*

Garlicky Brussels Sprouts

Ingredients

- ➢ 1 pound Brussels sprouts, halved
- ➢ 1 tablespoon olive oil
- ➢ Salt and black pepper, to taste
- ➢ ½ teaspoon sesame oil
- ➢ 1 garlic clove, minced
- ➢ ¼ cup coconut aminos
- ➢ ¼ cup of water

- ➢ 1 teaspoon apple cider vinegar
- ➢ ½ tablespoon Stevia
- ➢ 1 teaspoon garlic chili sauce
- ➢ ½ pinch red pepper flakes

How to prepare

1. Set a suitable cooking pot over medium heat.
2. Add olive oil, brussels sprouts, salt, black pepper, and red pepper flakes.
3. Sauté for 5 minutes, then stir in sesame oil, garlic clove, coconut aminos, water, apple cider, stevia, and garlic chili sauce.
4. Mix and cook for another 5 minutes.
5. Serve warm.

Preparation time: 10 minutes
Cooking time: 10 minutes
Total time: 20 minutes
Servings: 4

Nutritional Values

- ➢ *Calories 236*
- ➢ *Total Fat 21.5 g*
- ➢ *Saturated Fat 15.2 g*
- ➢ *Cholesterol 54 mg*

- *Total Carbs 7.6 g*
- *Sugar 1.4 g*
- *Fiber 3.8 g*
- *Sodium 21 mg*
- *Protein 4.3 g*

Roasted Cauliflower Florets

Ingredients

- ➤ 3 tablespoons olive oil
- ➤ Juice of 1 lime
- ➤ 2 tablespoons sweet chili sauce
- ➤ 1 pinch salt and black pepper
- ➤ 1 teaspoon cilantro, chopped
- ➤ 3 garlic cloves, minced
- ➤ 1 cauliflower head, florets separated

How to prepare

1. Set the oven for preheating at 350°F.

2. Toss the cauliflower florets with olive oil, lime juice, sweet chili sauce, salt, black pepper, garlic cloves and cilantro in a baking sheet.

3. Roast the florets for 7 minutes or more until golden-brown.

4. Serve warm.

Preparation time: 10 minutes

Cooking time: 7 minutes

Total time: 17 minutes

Servings: 6

Nutritional Values

- ➤ *Calories 167*
- ➤ *Total Fat 35.1 g*
- ➤ *Saturated Fat 10.1 g*
- ➤ *Cholesterol 12 mg*
- ➤ *Total Carbs 8.9 g*
- ➤ *Sugar 3.8 g*
- ➤ *Fiber 2.1 g*
- ➤ *Sodium 48 mg*
- ➤ *Protein 6.3 g*

Roasted Broccoli Florets

Ingredients

- ➤ 4 tablespoon olive oil
- ➤ 2 broccoli heads, florets separated
- ➤ 4 garlic cloves, minced
- ➤ 1 cup mozzarella, shredded
- ➤ ½ cup parmesan, grated
- ➤ 1 cup coconut cream
- ➤ 2 tablespoon parsley, chopped

How to prepare

1. Set the oven for preheating at 350°F.

2. Toss the broccoli florets with olive oil, garlic, mozzarella, parmesan, coconut cream, and parsley in a baking sheet.

3. Roast the florets for 20 minutes or more until golden-brown.

4. Serve warm.

Preparation time: 10 minutes

Cooking time: 20 minutes

Total time: 30 minutes

Servings: 8

Nutritional Values

- ➢ *Calories 175*
- ➢ *Total Fat 16 g*
- ➢ *Saturated Fat 2.1 g*
- ➢ *Cholesterol 0 mg*
- ➢ *Total Carbs 2.8 g*
- ➢ *Sugar 1.8 g*
- ➢ *Fiber 0.4 g*
- ➢ *Sodium 8 mg*
- ➢ *Protein 9 g*

Savory Bacon Brussels Sprouts

Ingredients

- ➢ 1 tablespoon parsley, chopped
- ➢ 1 pinch salt and black pepper
- ➢ 2 teaspoons sweet paprika
- ➢ 1 pound Brussels sprouts, halved
- ➢ 1 yellow onion, chopped
- ➢ 2 tablespoon Stevia

- 7 bacon slices, chopped
- 2 tablespoons olive oil

How to prepare

1. Set the oven for preheating at 350°F.
2. Toss the Brussels sprouts with onion, bacon, and rest of the ingredients in a baking sheet.
3. Roast the Brussels sprouts for 8 minutes.
4. Serve warm.

Preparation time: 10 minutes
Cooking time: 8 minutes
Total time: 18 minutes
Servings: 6

Nutritional Values

- *Calories 285*
- *Total Fat 27.3 g*
- *Saturated Fat 14.5 g*
- *Cholesterol 175 mg*
- *Total Carbs 3.5 g*
- *Sugar 0.4 g*
- *Fiber 0.9 g*
- *Sodium 165 mg*
- *Protein 7.2 g*

Cheesy Artichoke

Ingredients

- ➢ 7 ½ ounces canned artichoke hearts, drained
- ➢ Salt and black pepper, to taste
- ➢ 1 cup baby spinach
- ➢ 1 tablespoon parsley, chopped
- ➢ ½ cup mozzarella, shredded
- ➢ Juice of a ½ lemon
- ➢ 2/3 cup coconut milk
- ➢ ¼ cup chicken stock
- ➢ 1 garlic clove, minced
- ➢ 1 tablespoon ghee, melted

➤ ½ pinch red pepper flakes

How to prepare

1. Start by adding the cheesy artichoke ingredients to a suitable cooking pot.
2. Cover the pot with its lid and cook for about 10 minutes on a simmer with occasional stirring.
3. Mix well and garnish as desired.
4. Serve warm.

Preparation time: 10 minutes
Cooking time: 10 minutes
Total time: 20 minutes
Servings: 6

Nutritional Values

➤ *Calories 215*
➤ *Total Fat 20 g*
➤ *Saturated Fat 7 g*
➤ *Cholesterol 38 mg*
➤ *Total Carbs 8 g*
➤ *Sugar 1 g*
➤ *Fiber 6 g*
➤ *Sodium 12 mg*
➤ *Protein 5 g*

Cranberry Brussels Sprouts Salad

Ingredients

- ➤ 2 pounds Brussels sprouts, halved
- ➤ 4 tablespoons olive oil
- ➤ 2 teaspoons rosemary, chopped
- ➤ 2 tablespoons balsamic vinegar
- ➤ 2 teaspoons thyme, chopped
- ➤ 1 cup cranberries, dried

How to prepare

1. Toss the Brussels sprouts with all the salad ingredients in a salad bowl.
2. Serve.

Preparation time: 10 minutes

Cooking time: 0 minutes

Total time: 10 minutes

Servings: 6

Nutritional Values

- ➤ *Calories 198*
- ➤ *Total Fat 19.2 g*
- ➤ *Saturated Fat 11.5 g*
- ➤ *Cholesterol 123 mg*
- ➤ *Total Carbs 4.5 g*
- ➤ *Sugar 3.3 g*
- ➤ *Fiber 0.3 g*
- ➤ *Sodium 142 mg*
- ➤ *Protein 3.4 g*

Cauliflower Rice

Ingredients

- ➤ ½ tablespoon ghee, melted
- ➤ Juice of 1 lime
- ➤ Salt and black pepper, to taste
- ➤ ½ cup cauliflower rice
- ➤ 2/3 cup vegetable stock
- ➤ ½ tablespoon cilantro, chopped

How to prepare

1. Start by adding the cauliflower rice ingredients to a suitable cooking pot.
2. Cover the pot with its lid and cook for about 8 minutes on a simmer with occasional stirring.
3. Mix well and garnish as desired.
4. Serve warm.

Preparation time: 10 minutes

Cooking time: 8 minutes

Total time: 18 minutes

Servings: 2

Nutritional Values

➤ *Calories 288*
➤ *Total Fat 25.3 g*
➤ *Saturated Fat 6.7 g*
➤ *Cholesterol 23 mg*
➤ *Total Carbs 9.6 g*
➤ *Sugar 0.1 g*
➤ *Fiber 3.8 g*
➤ *Sodium 74 mg*
➤ *Protein 7.6 g*

Cauliflower Mash

Ingredients

- ➤ 1 cauliflower head, florets separated
- ➤ 1/6 cup coconut cream
- ➤ 1/6 cup coconut milk
- ➤ ½ tablespoon chives, chopped
- ➤ Salt and black pepper, to taste

How to prepare

1. Start by adding cauliflower and coconut milk to a suitable

cooking pot.

2. Cover the pot with its lid and cook for about 10 minutes on a simmer with occasional stirring.

3. Mash the cooked cauliflower in a mixing bowl and stir in coconut cream, chives, salt, and black pepper.

4. Mix well and garnish as desired.

5. Serve.

Preparation time: 10 minutes

Cooking time: 10 minutes

Total time: 20 minutes

Servings: 6

Nutritional Values

➢ *Calories 192*

➢ *Total Fat 17.44 g*

➢ *Saturated Fat 11.5 g*

➢ *Cholesterol 125 mg*

➢ *Total Carbs 2.2 g*

➢ *Sugar 1.4 g*

➢ *Fiber 2.1 g*

➢ *Sodium 135 mg*

➢ *Protein 4.7 g*

Chapter 9: Keto Dip Recipes

Kalamata Spinach Dip

Ingredients

- ➢ 4 cups baby spinach
- ➢ ½ cup coconut cream
- ➢ Salt and black pepper, to taste

- 4 garlic cloves, roasted and minced
- 1 cup kalamata olives, pitted and halved

How to prepare

1. Add olives and all other ingredients to a cooking pot.
2. Cover the pot with its lid and cook for 10 minutes on medium heat.
3. Use an immersion blender to blend the olives mixture until smooth.
4. Serve fresh and enjoy.

Preparation time: 10 minutes
Cooking time: 10 minutes
Total time: 20 minutes
Servings: 8

Nutritional Values

- *Calories 135*
- *Total Fat 9.9 g*
- *Saturated Fat 3.2 g*
- *Cholesterol 34 mg*
- *Sodium 10 mg*
- *Total Carbs 3.1 g*
- *Sugar 3.4 g*
- *Fiber 1.5 g*
- *Protein 8.6 g*

Mixed Peppers Dip

Ingredients

- ➤ 3 shallots, minced
- ➤ 1 ½ pounds mixed peppers, roughly chopped
- ➤ ¼ cup chicken stock
- ➤ 1 tablespoon olive oil
- ➤ 2 tablespoons basil, chopped

How to prepare

1. Start by sautéing shallots with oil in a pan, then sauté for

2 minutes.

2. Stir in remaining ingredients and mix well

3. Cover the pot with its lid and cook for 13 minutes on medium heat.

4. Use an immersion blender to blend the pepper mixture until smooth

5. Serve fresh and enjoy.

Preparation time: 10 minutes

Cooking time: 15 minutes

Total time: 25 minutes

Servings: 8

Nutritional Values

➤ *Calories 199*

➤ *Total Fat 17.4 g*

➤ *Saturated Fat 11.3 g*

➤ *Cholesterol 47 mg*

➤ *Sodium 192 mg*

➤ *Total Carbs 9.9 g*

➤ *Sugar 1.5 g*

➤ *Fiber 4.3 g*

➤ *Protein 6.4 g*

Watercress Avocado Salsa

Ingredients

- ➤ 1 bunch watercress, trimmed
- ➤ ¼ cup chicken stock
- ➤ 1 cup tomato, peeled and cubed
- ➤ 1 avocado; peeled, pitted, and cubed
- ➤ 2 zucchinis, cubed

How to prepare

1. Start by adding watercress and all other ingredients to a cooking pot.
2. Cover the pot with its lid and cook for 10 minutes on medium heat.
3. Serve fresh and enjoy.

Preparation time: 10 minutes

Cooking time: 10 minutes

Total time: 20 minutes

Servings: 8

Nutritional Values

- ➢ *Calories 279*
- ➢ *Total Fat 4.8 g*
- ➢ *Saturated Fat 1 g*
- ➢ *Cholesterol 45 mg*
- ➢ *Sodium 24 mg*
- ➢ *Total Carbs 5.8 g*
- ➢ *Sugar 2.3 g*
- ➢ *Fiber 4.5 g*
- ➢ *Protein 5 g*

Eggplant Spinach Dip

Ingredients

- ➢ 2 eggplants, cubed
- ➢ 1 cup baby spinach
- ➢ ¼ cup vegetable stock
- ➢ ¼ cup coconut cream
- ➢ Salt and black pepper, to taste

How to prepare

1. Add eggplants, spinach, and all other ingredients to a suitable cooking pot.
2. Cover the pot with its lid and cook for 15 minutes on medium heat.
3. Blend this mixture using a handheld blender until smooth.
4. Serve fresh and enjoy.

Preparation time: 10 minutes

Cooking time: 15 minutes

Total time: 25 minutes

Servings: 8

Nutritional Values

- ➢ *Calories 149*
- ➢ *Total Fat 14.5 g*
- ➢ *Saturated Fat 8.1 g*
- ➢ *Cholesterol 56 mg*
- ➢ *Sodium 56 mg*
- ➢ *Total Carbs 10.6 g*
- ➢ *Sugar 0.3 g*
- ➢ *Fiber 0.2 g*
- ➢ *Protein 2.6 g*

Walnuts Zucchinis Dip

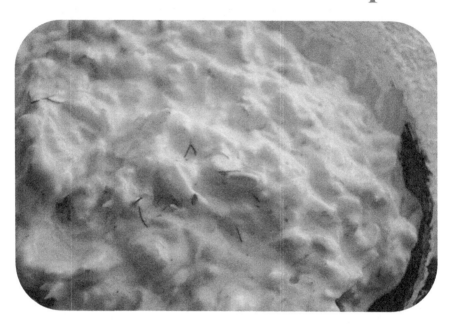

Ingredients

- ➢ 4 zucchinis, sliced
- ➢ ½ cup vegetable stock
- ➢ 3 garlic cloves, minced
- ➢ 1 cup walnuts, chopped
- ➢ ¼ cup parmesan cheese, grated

How to prepare

1. Add zucchinis and other ingredients (except for parmesan) to a cooking pot.
2. Cover the pot with its lid and cook for 12 minutes on medium heat.
3. Puree the mixture with hand blender.
4. Garnish with parmesan cheese.
5. Serve fresh and enjoy.

Preparation time: 10 minutes

Cooking time: 12 minutes

Total time: 22 minutes

Servings: 12

Nutritional Values

- *Calories 145*
- *Total Fat 13.1 g*
- *Saturated Fat 9.1 g*
- *Cholesterol 96 mg*
- *Sodium 35 mg*
- *Total Carbs 4 g*
- *Sugar 1.2 g*
- *Fiber 1.5 g*
- *Protein 3.5 g*

Artichokes Spinach Spread

Ingredients

- ➢ 14 ounces canned artichoke hearts, drained
- ➢ 8 ounces mozzarella cheese, shredded
- ➢ 1 pound spinach, torn
- ➢ ½ cup chicken stock
- ➢ ½ cup coconut cream
- ➢ Salt and black pepper, to taste

How to prepare

1. Start by adding all ingredients for the spread to the Instant Pot.

2. Cover the pot with its lid and cook for 15 minutes on medium heat.

3. Blend the spinach mixture using a handheld blender until smooth.

4. Serve fresh and enjoy.

Preparation time: 10 minutes

Cooking time: 15 minutes

Total time: 25 minutes

Servings: 12

Nutritional Values

➤ *Calories 255*

➤ *Total Fat 23.4 g*

➤ *Saturated Fat 11.7 g*

➤ *Cholesterol 135 mg*

➤ *Sodium 112 mg*

➤ *Total Carbs 2.5 g*

➤ *Sugar 12.5 g*

➤ *Fiber 1 g*

➤ *Protein 27.9 g*

Mustard Greens Dip

Ingredients

- ➢ 6 ounces mustard greens, chopped
- ➢ 1 tablespoon olive oil
- ➢ 1 tablespoon basil, chopped
- ➢ ¼ cup vegetable stock
- ➢ 2 tablespoons coconut cream
- ➢ Salt and black pepper, to taste

How to prepare:

1. Start by tossing in all the ingredients to a cooking pot.
2. Cover the pot with its lid and cook for 13 minutes on medium heat.
3. Blend the greens mixture with a handheld blender until smooth.
4. Serve fresh and enjoy.

Preparation time: 10 minutes
Cooking time: 13 minutes
Total time: 23 minutes
Servings: 8

Nutritional Values

- *Calories 307*
- *Total Fat 29 g*
- *Saturated Fat 14g*
- *Cholesterol 111 mg*
- *Sodium 122 mg*
- *Total Carbs 7 g*
- *Sugar 1 g*
- *Fiber 3 g*
- *Protein 6 g*

Avocado Tomato Salsa

Ingredients

- ➤ 2 cups red radishes, sliced
- ➤ 2 spring onions, chopped
- ➤ 2 tomatoes, cubed
- ➤ 1 avocado, peeled and cubed
- ➤ 1 tablespoon olive oil
- ➤ Salt and black pepper, to taste

How to prepare

1. Start by tossing radishes with all the ingredients on a baking tray.
2. Bake them for about 5 minutes in a preheated oven at 350°F.
3. Serve fresh and enjoy.

Preparation time: 10 minutes

Cooking time: 5 minutes

Total time: 15 minutes

Servings: 8

Nutritional Values

- *Calories 267*
- *Total Fat 44.5 g*
- *Saturated Fat 17.4 g*
- *Cholesterol 153 mg*
- *Sodium 217 mg*
- *Total Carbs 8.4 g*
- *Sugar 2.3 g*
- *Fiber 1.3 g*
- *Protein 3.1 g*

Cauliflower Spread

Ingredients

- ➢ 1 tablespoon avocado oil
- ➢ 2 tablespoons ginger, minced
- ➢ 1 pound cauliflower florets
- ➢ ¼ cup chicken stock
- ➢ 1 ¼ tablespoon balsamic vinegar

How to prepare

1. Add oil and ginger, to the cooking pot, then sauté for 2 minutes.

2. Stir in remaining ingredients and mix well

3. Cover the pot with its lid and cook for 13 minutes on medium heat.

4. Blend the cauliflower mixture with a handheld blender until smooth.

5. Serve fresh and enjoy.

Preparation time: 10 minutes

Cooking time: 15 minutes

Total time: 25 minutes

Servings: 8

Nutritional Values

- ➤ *Calories 331*
- ➤ *Total Fat 38.5 g*
- ➤ *Saturated Fat 19.2 g*
- ➤ *Cholesterol 141 mg*
- ➤ *Sodium 283 mg*
- ➤ *Total Carbs 9.2 g*
- ➤ *Sugar 3 g*
- ➤ *Fiber 1 g*
- ➤ *Protein 2.1 g*

Broccoli Yogurt Dip

Ingredients

- ➤ 2 cups vegetable stock
- ➤ 6 cups broccoli florets
- ➤ 1 cup Greek yogurt
- ➤ Salt and black pepper, to taste
- ➤ ½ cup coconut cream

How to prepare

1. Start by adding broccoli and all other ingredients to a

cooking pot.

2. Cover the pot with its lid and cook for 13 minutes on medium heat.

3. Add yogurt and blend the mixture with a handheld blender until smooth.

4. Serve fresh.

Preparation time: 10 minutes

Cooking time: 13 minutes

Total time: 23 minutes

Servings: 12

Nutritional Values

➤ *Calories 216*

➤ *Total Fat 10.9 g*

➤ *Saturated Fat 8.1 g*

➤ *Cholesterol 0 mg*

➤ *Sodium 8 mg*

➤ *Total Carbs 8.3 g*

➤ *Sugar 1.8 g*

➤ *Fiber 3.8 g*

➤ *Protein 6.4 g*

Chapter 10: Keto Pie Recipes

Pecan Chocolate Pie

Ingredients

Crust

- ➤ 6 tablespoons granulated Swerve
- ➤ 3 large eggs

- ➢ 6 tablespoons butter, unsalted, melted
- ➢ 2 2/3 cups almond flour
- ➢ 1 teaspoon salt

Filling

- ➢ 1 tablespoon bourbon
- ➢ ¾ cup butter, unsalted
- ➢ 1 tablespoon choc zero maple syrup
- ➢ ½ cup Swerve, brown
- ➢ ½ cup pecan, cut in half
- ➢ ¼ teaspoon salt
- ➢ ½ cup granulated Swerve
- ➢ 3 large eggs
- ➢ ¾ cup sugar-free chocolate chips
- ➢ 1 cup pecan, chopped

How to prepare

Crust

1. Let your oven preheat at 325°F.
2. Grease a 10-inch baking pan with butter.
3. Mix all the pecan pie crust ingredients in a bowl to form a dough.
4. Place this dough crust in the prepared pan and bake it for 15 minutes.

Filling

5. Melt butter in a pan and dissolve swerve in it. Allow it to

cool.

6. Beat eggs in a suitable bowl and stir in butter mixture, salt, bourbon, chocolate chips, maple flavoring, and chopped pecan.

7. Pour this filling in the baked crust and top this filling with halved pecan.

8. Bake the pie for 40 minutes in the preheated oven.

9. Slice and serve.

Preparation time: 10 minutes
Cooking time: 55 minutes
Total time: 65 minutes
Servings: 8

Nutritional Values

- ➤ *Calories 237*
- ➤ *Total Fat 22 g*
- ➤ *Saturated Fat 9 g*
- ➤ *Cholesterol 35 mg*
- ➤ *Total Carbs 5 g*
- ➤ *Sugar 1 g*
- ➤ *Fiber 2 g*
- ➤ *Sodium 118 mg*
- ➤ *Protein 5 g*

Cream Cheese Samoa Pie

Ingredients

Chocolate Crust

- ½ cup sunflower seeds raw, unsalted
- ½ cup sugar-free cocoa powder
- ½ cup coconut flour
- ½ cup Swerve
- ½ teaspoon salt
- 8 tablespoon butter soft

Filling

- 16 ounces heavy whipping cream
- 1 teaspoon vanilla liquid Stevia
- 8 ounces cream cheese softened

Topping

- ½ cup coconut flakes sugar-free, toasted
- 2 ounces sugar-free chocolate chips, melted
- 3 teaspoons butter

How to prepare

1. Add and blend all the ingredients for the crust in a food processor.
2. Pulse the processor to blend everything together until smooth.
3. Spread this mixture into a 9-inch pie pan and press it down. Set it aside.
4. Beat heavy cream with Stevia and vanilla in a bowl.
5. Whisk the cream cheese in an electric mixer and stir in cream mixture.
6. Mix well, then spread this filling into the pie crust.
7. Toss coconut flakes with chocolate and butter in a bowl to prepare the topping.
8. Drizzle melted chocolate mixture over the filling.
9. Refrigerate the pie for 3 hours.

10. Slice and serve.

Preparation time: 10 minutes

Cooking time: 0 minutes

Total time: 10 minutes

Servings: 8

Nutritional Values

- ➢ *Calories 190*
- ➢ *Total Fat 17.25 g*
- ➢ *Saturated Fat 7.1 g*
- ➢ *Cholesterol 20 mg*
- ➢ *Total Carbs 5.5 g*
- ➢ *Sugar 2.8 g*
- ➢ *Fiber 3.8 g*
- ➢ *Sodium 28 mg*
- ➢ *Protein 3 g*

Strawberry Cream Pie

Ingredients

Shortbread Crust

- 1 ½ cups almond flour
- ¼ cup powdered Swerve Sweetener
- ¼ teaspoon salt
- ¼ cup butter, melted

Strawberry Cream Filling

- 1 cup heavy whipping cream

- 1 ½ cups fresh strawberries, chopped
- ¼ cup water
- 2 ½ teaspoon gelatine, grass-fed
- ½ cup powdered Swerve Sweetener
- ¾ teaspoon vanilla essence
- Whipped cream for serving

How to prepare

1. Mix almond flour with salt and sweetener in a medium bowl.
2. Whisk in melted butter and mix well to form a coarse mixture.
3. Spread this mixture in a pie plate.
4. Spread the crust mixture into the plate and press it firmly.
5. Freeze crust until the filling is prepared.

Strawberry Cream Filling

6. Puree all the chopped strawberries in a blender or food processor with water.
7. Cook this puree with gelatine in a saucepan on low heat.
8. Bring the heat to a low then turn off the heat. Allow it to cool for 20 minutes.
9. Beat cream with vanilla essence and sweetener in a suitable bowl.

10. Stir in strawberry mixture and mix well until smooth.

11. Spread this mixture into the frozen crust.

12. Refrigerate this pie for 3 hours.

13. Garnish with whipped cream and berries.

14. Serve.

Preparation time: 10 minutes

Cooking time: 5 minutes

Total time: 15 minutes

Servings: 8

Nutritional Values

- ➤ *Calories 321*
- ➤ *Total Fat 12.9 g*
- ➤ *Saturated Fat 5.1 g*
- ➤ *Cholesterol 17 mg*
- ➤ *Total Carbs 8.1 g*
- ➤ *Sugar 1.8 g*
- ➤ *Fiber 0.4 g*
- ➤ *Sodium 28 mg*
- ➤ *Protein 5.4 g*

Blueberry Cream Pie

Ingredients

Crust

- ➤ ½ tablespoon water
- ➤ ½ cup butter, unsalted and melted
- ➤ 2 large eggs
- ➤ ¼ teaspoon salt

- ➤ ¾ cup coconut flour
- ➤ 1/8 teaspoon baking powder

Filling

- ➤ 1 tablespoon swerve
- ➤ ¾ cup blueberries
- ➤ 8 ounces cream cheese

How to prepare

Crust

1. Prepare the crust dough by mixing all of the crust ingredients.
2. Divide this dough into two equal halves.
3. Roll both the halves into two 6-inch-round sheets.
4. Place one sheet in a greased 6-inch pie plate and set the pan aside.

Pie

5. Let your oven preheat at 350°F.
6. Spread cream cheese over the base layer of the crust.
7. Mix blueberries with 2 tablespoons sweeteners in a bowl.
8. Spread this berry mixture over the cream cheese layer.
9. Place the other sheet of the dough on top of the filling.
10. Press and pinch the dough around the edges to seal the

pie.

11. Bake the pie for 25 minutes in the preheated oven.

12. Allow the baked pie to cool at room temperature.

13. Slice and serve.

Preparation time: 10 minutes

Cooking time: 25 minutes

Total time: 35 minutes

Servings: 8

Nutritional Values

➢ *Calories 236*

➢ *Total Fat 21.5 g*

➢ *Saturated Fat 15.2 g*

➢ *Cholesterol 54 mg*

➢ *Total Carbs 7.6 g*

➢ *Sugar 1.4 g*

➢ *Fiber 3.8 g*

➢ *Sodium 21 mg*

➢ *Protein 4.3 g*

Vanilla Cheesecake Pie

Ingredients

Crust

- ➤ 3 tablespoons butter, melted
- ➤ ¾ cup almond flour

Filling

- ➤ 12 ounces cream cheese, room temperature

- ➢ 1 egg
- ➢ ¼ cup erythritol
- ➢ 1 teaspoon vanilla essence
- ➢ 1 tablespoon fresh lemon juice
- ➢ ¼ teaspoon salt

How to prepare

1. Let your oven preheat at 350°F.
2. Mix melted butter with almond flour in a bowl until it forms a coarse mixture.
3. Layer a muffin tray with cupcake liners and press 2 teaspoons of this mixture in the muffin cups.
4. Bake these crusts for 8 minutes in the preheated oven until golden.
5. Beat cream cheese in an electric mixer.
6. Add all the remaining filling ingredients and continue beating.
7. Divide this filling in the baked crusts.
8. Bake again for 20 minutes. Allow the cakes to cool.
9. Refrigerate well then serve.

Preparation time: 10 minutes

Cooking time: 28 minutes

Total time: 38 minutes

Servings: 8

Nutritional Values

- ➢ Calories 367
- ➢ Total Fat 35.1 g
- ➢ Saturated Fat 10.1 g
- ➢ Cholesterol 12 mg
- ➢ Total Carbs 8.9 g
- ➢ Sugar 3.8 g
- ➢ Fiber 2.1 g
- ➢ Sodium 48 mg
- ➢ Protein 6.3 g

Chocolate Pie

Ingredients

Crust

- ➢ 6 tablespoons almond flour
- ➢ 2 tablespoons erythritol
- ➢ 4 tablespoons butter, melted
- ➢ 1 8-inch pie pan
- ➢ 1 large egg

Filling

- 1 large egg
- 2 ounces sugar-free chocolate, shredded
- ½ cup heavy whipping cream
- 30 drops liquid Stevia
- ¼ cup erythritol powder
- 1 ounce cream cheese

How to prepare:

1. Let your oven preheat at 350°F.
2. Mix all the crust ingredients in a mixing bowl.
3. Spread this mixture into the pie pan and press it well.
4. Poke some holes in the crust, then bake it for 12 minutes.
5. Allow this crust to cool until the filling is ready.
6. Warm the cream up in a saucepan, then pour it into a jar.
7. Add chopped chocolate and blend well using a hand blender.
8. Stir in Stevia, erythritol, egg, and cream cheese. Blend well until smooth.
9. Spread this filling into the baked crust and return the pie to the oven.
10. Bake them for 15 minutes at 325°F.
11. Allow them to cool then refrigerate for 2 hours.
12. Serve.

Preparation time: 10 minutes

Cooking time: 27 minutes

Total time: 37 minutes

Servings: 8

Nutritional Values

- *Calories 175*
- *Total Fat 16 g*
- *Saturated Fat 2.1 g*
- *Cholesterol 0 mg*
- *Total Carbs 2.8 g*
- *Sugar 1.8 g*
- *Fiber 0.4 g*
- *Sodium 8 mg*
- *Protein 9 g*

Strawberry Cheesecake Pie

Ingredients

Crust

- ➢ 2 cups almond flour
- ➢ ¼ cup + 1 tablespoon granulated Swerve
- ➢ 3 ounces butter

Cheesecake Filling

- ➢ 1 cup cream cheese
- ➢ ½ cup heavy whipping cream
- ➢ ¼ cup + 1 tablespoon confectioners Swerve
- ➢ ½ teaspoon sugar-free vanilla essence

Berry Topping

- ➢ 1 cup strawberries
- ➢ 1 teaspoon granulated Swerve
- ➢ ¼ teaspoon sugar-free vanilla essence

How to prepare

1. Let your oven preheat at 350°F.
2. Mix almond meal with melted butter and sweetener in a bowl to form a coarse mixture.
3. Grease one 9-inch pie pan and spread the crust mixture into the pan.
4. Poke some holes in the crust then bake them for 15 minutes almost.
5. Allow the baked pie crust to cool at room temperature.
6. Toss strawberries pieces with vanilla and sweetener in a bowl then spread them in a baking tray.
7. Bake the berries for 20 minutes then allow them to cool.
8. Beat cream cheese with vanilla and sweetener in an electric mixer until fluffy.
9. Stir in cream and continue beating until creamy.

10. Pass one-half of the strawberries through a sieve to remove all the seeds.

11. Add this berry puree to the cream cheese mixture and mix gently to make swirls.

12. Spread this filling mixture in the crust.

13. Refrigerate the pie for 1 hour.

14. Top it with remaining berries.

15. Serve.

Preparation time: 10 minutes

Cooking time: 35 minutes

Total time: 45 minutes

Servings: 8

Nutritional Values

➢ *Calories 285*

➢ *Total Fat 27.3 g*

➢ *Saturated Fat 14.5 g*

➢ *Cholesterol 175 mg*

➢ *Total Carbs 3.5 g*

➢ *Sugar 0.4 g*

➢ *Fiber 0.9 g*

➢ *Sodium 165 mg*

➢ *Protein 7.2 g*

Cranberry Curd Pie

Ingredients

Shortbread Tart Crust

- ➤ 1 cup blanched almond flour
- ➤ 4 tablespoons salted butter
- ➤ 1 tablespoon Swerve
- ➤ 1 teaspoon vanilla

Keto Cranberry Curd

- ➤ 2 ½ cups cranberries

- ➤ ½ cup of water
- ➤ 6 tablespoons salted butter
- ➤ ¼ cup Swerve
- ➤ 4 egg yolks
- ➤ ½ teaspoon vanilla

How to prepare

Keto Shortbread Crust

1. Let your oven preheat at 350°F. Grease an 8-inch pie pan.
2. Beat all the ingredients for the crust in an electric mixer to form a smooth dough.
3. Spread this dough in the greased pie pan.
4. Poke some holes in the pie crust and bake it for 15 minutes.
5. Set it aside to cool until filling is ready.

Keto Cranberry Curd

6. Boil cranberries with water in a saucepan then reduce the heat to a simmer.
7. Allow this berry mixture to cool for 5 minutes while smashing the cranberries using a wooden spoon.
8. Pass this berry mixture through a sieve to remove the seeds.
9. This will give 1 cup cranberry puree.

10. Heat this puree in a saucepan then add salt, sweetener, and butter.

11. Mix well, then remove it from the heat.

12. Once cooled, whisk in vanilla and egg yolks. Mix well until smooth.

13. Pour this filling in the baked crust.

14. Refrigerate them for 30 minutes.

15. Serve.

Preparation time: 10 minutes

Cooking time: 25 minutes

Total time: 35 minutes

Servings: 8

Nutritional Values

➢ *Calories 215*

➢ *Total Fat 20 g*

➢ *Saturated Fat 7 g*

➢ *Cholesterol 38 mg*

➢ *Sodium 12 mg*

➢ *Total Carbs 8 g*

➢ *Sugar 1 g*

➢ *Fiber 6 g*

➢ *Protein 5 g*

Chapter 11: Keto Dessert Recipes

Zesty Keto Custard

Ingredients

- ➤ 2 teaspoons xylitol
- ➤ 4 egg yolks
- ➤ ¼ teaspoon ground vanilla bean
- ➤ ¾ cup whipping/pouring cream

➢ 1 teaspoon xanthan gum

Optional Flavors

➢ 1 teaspoon raw cacao

➢ ½ teaspoon lemon zest

How to prepare

1. Beat sweetener with egg yolks, xanthan gum, and vanilla until pale in color.
2. Boil cream in a saucepan then whisks in yolk mixture gradually while stirring.
3. Remove the cooked custard from the heat and continue stirring for 1 minute.
4. Allow it to cool, then garnish with cocoa or lemon zest.
5. Enjoy.

Preparation time: 10 minutes

Cooking time: 10 minutes

Total time: 20 minutes

Servings: 4

Nutritional Values

➢ *Calories 243*

➢ *Total Fat 21 g*

➢ *Saturated Fat 18.2 g*

- *Cholesterol 121 mg*
- *Total Carbs 7.3 g*
- *Sugar 0.9 g*
- *Fiber 0.1 g*
- *Sodium 34 mg*
- *Protein 4.3 g*

Lemon Custard

Ingredients

- 2 cups heavy cream
- 2 tablespoons lemon zest
- 6 large eggs
- Sliced lemons for topping
- 1 cup granulated Swerve

How to prepare

1. Let your oven preheat at 300°F.
2. Blend all the custard ingredients in a bowl using a hand

mixer for 1 minute.

3. Divide this mixture into two half-cup ramekins.

4. Set these ramekins in a baking pan.

5. Pour in enough hot water to the pan to cover the ¾ of the ramekins.

6. Bake them for 50 minutes.

7. Allow the hot ramekins to cool at room temperature then refrigerate for 2 hours.

8. Garnish with lemon slices.

9. Enjoy.

Preparation time: 10 minutes

Cooking time: 50 minutes

Total time: 60 minutes

Servings: 2

Nutritional Values

➢ *Calories 183*

➢ *Total Fat 15 g*

➢ *Saturated Fat 12.1 g*

➢ *Cholesterol 11 mg*

➢ *Total Carbs 6.2 g*

➢ *Sugar 1.6 g*

➢ *Fiber 0.8 g*

➢ *Sodium 31 mg*

➢ *Protein 4.5 g*

Mocha Coffee Custards

Ingredients

- ½ cup heavy cream
- ¼ cup coffee, black
- 3 egg yolks
- 1 tablespoon granulated swerve
- 1.8 ounce 90% dark chocolate

How to prepare

1. Warm up the cream in a saucepan with chocolate pieces and coffee on a simmer.

2. Then remove them from heat.

3. Beat egg yolks with sweetener in a mixer until fluffy and pale in color.

4. Gradually pour this mixture into the cream mixture while mixing gently.

5. Return the saucepan to low heat and stir cook until it thickens.

6. Divide into cups and refrigerate until the custard is set.

7. Serve.

Preparation time: 10 minutes

Cooking time: 10 minutes

Total time: 20 minutes

Servings: 4

Nutritional Values

➢ *Calories 388*

➢ *Total Fat 31 g*

➢ *Saturated Fat 12.2 g*

➢ *Cholesterol 101 mg*

➢ *Total Carbs 3 g*

➢ *Sugar 1.3 g*

➢ *Fiber 0.6 g*

➢ *Sodium 54 mg*

➢ *Protein 5 g*

Berry Creme Brulee

Ingredients

Brûlée

- ➢ 5 egg yolks
- ➢ 1 teaspoon vanilla essence
- ➢ 1/8 teaspoon salt
- ➢ 1/3 cup granulated Swerve
- ➢ 2 cups heavy cream

Filling

- ➢ 1/3 cup water

- ➤ 1/3 cup granulated Swerve
- ➤ 1 cup fresh blueberries

How to prepare

Filling

1. Mix water, swerve, and blueberries in a cooking pot over medium-high heat.
2. Let it boil then cook it on a simmer until it thickens.
3. Remove the blueberry pan from the heat and allow it to cool.

Brulee

4. Warm heavy cream with salt in a cooking pan over medium heat on low heat until it bubbles.
5. Remove it from the heat then add vanilla.
6. Meanwhile, beat egg yolks with swerve in an electric mixer until creamy.
7. Add 1/3 cream into egg yolks mixture and mix well.
8. Return this mixture to the cream while mixing well.

Assemble

9. Let your oven preheat at 350°F.
10. Divide the blueberry sauce in the two ramekins.
11. Divide the custard over this filling in each ramekin.

12. Bake them for 40 minutes in the preheated oven.

13. Allow it to cool then refrigerate for 2 hours or more.

14. Serve.

Preparation time: 10 minutes

Cooking time: 50 minutes

Total time: 60 minutes

Servings: 2

Nutritional Values

- ➤ *Calories 153*
- ➤ *Total Fat 13 g*
- ➤ *Saturated Fat 9.2 g*
- ➤ *Cholesterol 6.5 mg*
- ➤ *Total Carbs 4.5 g*
- ➤ *Sugar 1.4 g*
- ➤ *Fiber 0.4 g*
- ➤ *Sodium 81 mg*
- ➤ *Protein 5.8 g*

Peanut Butter Mousse

Ingredients

- ½ cup heavy whipping cream
- 4 ounces cream cheese, softened
- ¼ cup peanut butter
- ¼ cup powdered Swerve Sweetener
- ½ teaspoon vanilla essence

How to prepare

1. Beat ½ cup cream in a mixer until it forms stiff peaks.
2. Take cream cheese in another bowl and blend it with peanut butter.
3. Add vanilla, salt, and sweetener while beating this mixture.
4. Fold in whipped cream and then divide this mixture into serving glasses.
5. Garnish with chocolate sauce.
6. Enjoy.

Preparation time: 10 minutes

Cooking time: 0 minutes

Total time: 10 minutes

Servings: 2

Nutritional Values

➢ *Calories 254*

➢ *Total Fat 09 g*

➢ *Saturated Fat 10.1 g*

➢ *Cholesterol 13 mg*

➢ *Total Carbs 7.5 g*

➢ *Sugar 1.2 g*

➢ *Fiber 0.8 g*

➢ *Sodium 179 mg*

➢ *Protein 7.5 g*

Chocolate Mousse

Ingredients

- ➢ 1 ¼ cup coconut cream
- ➢ ¼ cup heavy cream
- ➢ 2 tablespoons cocoa sugar-free
- ➢ 3 tablespoons erythritol
- ➢ 1 teaspoon vanilla essence

How to prepare

1. Blend all the ingredients in a mixer on low speed until it is thick.

2. Divide the mousse in the ramekins.

3. Garnish as desired.

4. Serve.

Preparation time: 10 minutes

Cooking time: 0 minutes

Total time: 10 minutes

Servings: 2

Nutritional Values

- ➤ *Calories 265*
- ➤ *Total Fat 13 g*
- ➤ *Saturated Fat 10.2 g*
- ➤ *Cholesterol 09 mg*
- ➤ *Total Carbs 7.5 g*
- ➤ *Sugar 1.1 g*
- ➤ *Fiber 0.5 g*
- ➤ *Sodium 7.1 mg*
- ➤ *Protein 5.2 g*

Cheesecake Fluff

Ingredients

- ➢ 1/3 cup erythritol powder
- ➢ 8 ounces cream cheese
- ➢ 1/8 teaspoon stevia powder
- ➢ 1 ½ teaspoons vanilla essence
- ➢ ¼ teaspoon lemon extract
- ➢ 1 cup heavy whipping cream

How to prepare

1. Beat the cream cheese in an electric mixer until smooth.

2. Whisk in lemon extract, vanilla, stevia, and erythritol. Mix well and set it aside.

3. Beat cream in the mixer until it forms peaks.

4. Slowly fold in cream cheese mixture. Continue beating until fluffy.

5. Refrigerate it for 2 hours.

6. Serve.

Preparation time: 10 minutes

Cooking time: 0 minutes

Total time: 10 minutes

Servings: 2

Nutritional Values

➢ *Calories 306*

➢ *Total Fat 30.8 g*

➢ *Saturated Fat 19.3 g*

➢ *Cholesterol 103 mg*

➢ *Total Carbs 4.6 g*

➢ *Sugar 0.3 g*

➢ *Fiber 0 g*

➢ *Sodium 179 mg*

➢ *Protein 4.9 g*

Cheesecake Tarts

Ingredients

Crust

- ➤ 2 cups coconut flour
- ➤ ¼ cup 1 tablespoon granulated Swerve
- ➤ 3 ounces butter

Cheesecake Filling

- ➢ 1 cup cream cheese
- ➢ ½ cup heavy whipping cream
- ➢ ¼ cup 1 tablespoon confectioners Swerve
- ➢ ½ teaspoon sugar-free vanilla essence

How to prepare

1. Let your oven preheat at 350°F.
2. Mix coconut flour with melted butter and sweetener in a bowl to form a coarse mixture.
3. Grease 6 mini tart pans and divides the crust mixture into the tart pans.
4. Poke some holes in each crust then bake them for approximately 15 minutes.
5. Allow the crust to cool at room temperature.
6. Beat cream cheese with vanilla and sweetener in an electric mixer until fluffy.
7. Stir in cream and continue beating until creamy.
8. Divide this mixture into the tart crusts.
9. Refrigerate the tarts for 1 hour.
10. Serve.

Preparation time: 10 minutes

Cooking time: 15 minutes

Total time: 25 minutes

Servings: 8

Nutritional Values

- ➤ *Calories 285*
- ➤ *Total Fat 27.3 g*
- ➤ *Saturated Fat 14.5 g*
- ➤ *Cholesterol 175 mg*
- ➤ *Total Carbs 3.5 g*
- ➤ *Sugar 0.4 g*
- ➤ *Fiber 0.9 g*
- ➤ *Sodium 165 mg*
- ➤ *Protein 7.2 g*

Strawberry Curd Tart

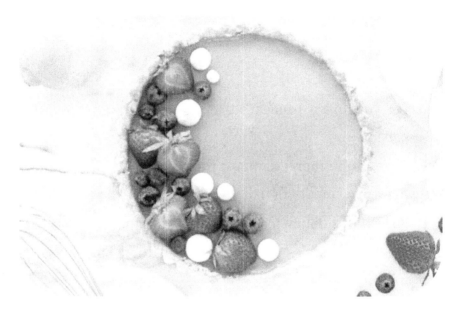

Ingredients

Shortbread Tart Crust

- ➢ 1 cup almond flour
- ➢ 4 tablespoons salted butter
- ➢ 1 tablespoon Swerve
- ➢ 1 teaspoon vanilla

Keto Cranberry Curd

- ➢ 1 strawberries puree

- ½ cup of water
- 6 tablespoons salted butter
- ¼ cup Swerve
- 4 egg yolks
- ½ teaspoon vanilla

How to prepare

Tart Crust

1. Let your oven preheat at 350°F. Grease an 8-inch tart pan.
2. Beat all the ingredients for the crust in an electric mixer to form a smooth dough.
3. Spread this dough in the greased tart pan.
4. Poke some holes in the crust and then bake it for 15 minutes.
5. Set it aside to cool until filling is ready.

Keto Strawberry Curd

6. Heat the strawberry puree in a saucepan then add salt, sweetener, and butter.
7. Mix well, then remove it from the heat.
8. Once cooled, whisk in vanilla and egg yolks. Mix well until smooth.
9. Pour this filling in the baked crust.

10. Refrigerate them for 30 minutes.

11. Serve.

Preparation time: 10 minutes

Cooking time: 15 minutes

Total time: 25 minutes

Servings: 8

Nutritional Values

- ➢ *Calories 215*
- ➢ *Total Fat 20 g*
- ➢ *Saturated Fat 7 g*
- ➢ *Cholesterol 38 mg*
- ➢ *Total Carbs 8 g*
- ➢ *Sugar 1 g*
- ➢ *Fiber 6 g*
- ➢ *Sodium 12 mg*
- ➢ *Protein 5 g*

Part 4: Holiday Keto Drinks

Chapter 12: Holiday Keto Hot Drinks

Keto Eggnog

Ingredients

- ¾ cup erythritol
- 1 cup heavy cream
- 2 teaspoon pure vanilla extract
- 2 cinnamon sticks, broken
- ¼ teaspoon freshly grated nutmeg
- 4 cup almond milk
- 8 large eggs, separated
- Pinch of kosher salt
- 1 cup dark rum

How to prepare

1. Add 2 cups almond milk, nutmeg, cinnamon, vanilla, and heavy cream to a saucepan.
2. Place it over medium heat and cook for 3 minutes on a simmer.
3. Remove it from the heat and leave it for 30 minutes.
4. Beat all the egg yolks in an electric mixer until smooth and creamy.
5. Stir in salt and erythritol, then beat again for 3 minutes.
6. Strain the cream sugar mixture and return to the pot.
7. Add egg yolks mixture and beat on low heat until incorporated.
8. Stir and chill the mixture for 30 minutes.
9. Add bourbon, and 2 cups milk then mix well.

10. Beat all the egg whites in an electric mixer until foamy.

11. Add the egg whites to the eggnog mixture.

12. Mix well for 2 minutes then garnish with nutmeg.

13. Serve.

Preparation time: 10 minutes

Cooking time: 6 minutes

Total time: 16 minutes

Servings: 10

Nutritional Values

- ➤ *Calories 187*
- ➤ *Total Fat 11.6 g*
- ➤ *Saturated Fat 5.8 g*
- ➤ *Cholesterol 175 mg*
- ➤ *Sodium 115 mg*
- ➤ *Total Carbohydrates 10.2 g*
- ➤ *Dietary Fiber 0 g*
- ➤ *Sugars 0.6 g*
- ➤ *Protein 8.4 g*

Keto Spiced Eggnog

Ingredients

- ➢ 1 (15-ounce) can coconut milk
- ➢ 2 cups almond milk
- ➢ 5 egg yolks
- ➢ 1/3 cup choc zero maple syrup
- ➢ ½ teaspoon ground cinnamon
- ➢ Pinch of salt

- ➢ 2 chai tea bags
- ➢ 1 teaspoon vanilla extract

How to prepare

1. Add coconut milk, egg yolks, almond milk, cinnamon, maple syrup, and salt to a large saucepan.
2. Place the pan over medium heat and mix well.
3. Cook until the mixture bubbles then reduce the heat.
4. Add tea bags and cook for 3 minutes with occasional stirring.
5. Discard the tea bags and add vanilla to the mixture.
6. Stir in maple syrup and mix well.
7. Serve.

Preparation time: 10 minutes
Cooking time: 6 minutes
Total time: 16 minutes
Servings: 4

Nutritional Values

- ➢ *Calories 103*
- ➢ *Total Fat 6.9 g*
- ➢ *Saturated Fat 2 g*
- ➢ *Cholesterol 262 mg*
- ➢ *Sodium 119 mg*

- ➤ *Total Carbohydrates 5.4 g*
- ➤ *Dietary Fiber 0.4 g*
- ➤ *Total Sugars 3.3 g*
- ➤ *Protein 4 g*

Low-Carb Hot Chocolate

Ingredients

- ➤ 2/3 cup granulated Swerve
- ➤ 6 tablespoons cocoa powder
- ➤ 1 tablespoon xanthan gum
- ➤ 3 ½ cups almond milk
- ➤ ½ cup heavy cream
- ➤ ½ teaspoon vanilla extract

How to prepare

1. In a suitable saucepan, mix cocoa powder, Swerve, and xanthan gum.
2. Stir in almond milk, then beat until well blended.
3. Cook this mixture to a boil and reduce the heat to low.
4. Continue cooking for 1 minute then add vanilla and cream.
5. Serve.

Preparation time: 10 minutes

Cooking time: 5 minutes

Total time: 15 minutes

Servings: 4

Nutritional Values

- ➢ *Calories 105*
- ➢ *Total Fat 7.2 g*
- ➢ *Saturated Fat 4.1 g*
- ➢ *Cholesterol 21 mg*
- ➢ *Sodium 887 mg*
- ➢ *Total Carbohydrates 7.5 g*
- ➢ *Dietary Fiber 27.4 g*
- ➢ *Total Sugars 1.7 g*
- ➢ *Protein 4 g*

Zesty Almond Milk Tea

Ingredients

- ➤ 8 ounces sweetened vanilla almond milk
- ➤ 1 teaspoon orange zest
- ➤ 1 ½ teaspoons loose leaf chai tea
- ➤ 1 ounce whiskey
- ➤ Cinnamon stick for garnish

How to prepare

1. Add almond milk and orange zest to a saucepan and place it over medium heat.

2. Cook the milk to a boil for 3 minutes, then add tea.

3. Add whiskey to milk.

4. Strain the tea and add cinnamon.

5. Garnish.

6. Serve.

Preparation time: 10 minutes
Cooking time: 3 minutes
Total time: 13 minutes
Servings: 2

Nutritional Values

➤ *Calories 85*
➤ *Total Fat 1.2 g*
➤ *Saturated Fat 0 g*
➤ *Cholesterol 0 mg*
➤ *Sodium 71 mg*
➤ *Total Carbohydrates 9.2 g*
➤ *Dietary Fiber 0.5 g*
➤ *Sugars 8.4 g*
➤ *Protein 0.6 g*

Spiced Hot Chocolate

Ingredients

- ➢ 4 cups almond milk
- ➢ 2 ½ cup half-and-half cream
- ➢ 2 cinnamon sticks
- ➢ 2 teaspoons cocoa powder
- ➢ 10 ounces sugar-free dark chocolate
- ➢ 2 teaspoon pure vanilla extract
- ➢ ¼ teaspoon Kosher salt
- ➢ ½ cup bourbon

How to prepare

1. Add and mix all the hot chocolate ingredients in a saucepan.
2. Cook for 8 minutes on low heat.
3. Strain and serve hot.

Preparation time: 10 minutes

Cooking time: 8 minutes

Total time: 18 minutes

Servings: 4

Nutritional Values

- ➢ *Calories 214*
- ➢ *Total Fat 12.7 g*
- ➢ *Saturated Fat 7.7 g*
- ➢ *Cholesterol 40 mg*
- ➢ *Sodium 170 mg*
- ➢ *Total Carbohydrates 6.6 g*
- ➢ *Dietary Fiber 0.6 g*
- ➢ *Sugars 1.3 g*
- ➢ *Protein 6.9 g*

Strawberry Tea

Ingredients

- ➢ 2 cups of water
- ➢ 2 teaspoon green whole leaf tea
- ➢ 4 strawberries, sliced

How to prepare

1. Add all the tea ingredients to a pan and cook for 5

minutes.

2. Leave them for 5 minutes then strain the liquid.

3. Garnish with strawberry slices.

4. Serve.

Preparation time: 10 minutes

Cooking time: 5 minutes

Total time: 15 minutes

Servings: 2

Nutritional Values

- ➤ *Calories 8*
- ➤ *Total Fat 0.1 g*
- ➤ *Saturated Fat 0 g*
- ➤ *Cholesterol 0 mg*
- ➤ *Sodium 8 mg*
- ➤ *Total Carbohydrates 1.8 g*
- ➤ *Dietary Fiber 0.5 g*
- ➤ *Total Sugars 1.2 g*
- ➤ *Protein 0.2 g*

Coconut Vanilla Drink

Ingredients

- ➤ 3 ounces white rum
- ➤ 1 ½ cups almond milk
- ➤ ½ cup canned coconut milk
- ➤ 1 ½ teaspoon coconut extract
- ➤ 1 vanilla bean
- ➤ Toasted coconut for garnish

How to prepare

1. Add and mix all the vanilla steamer ingredients in a saucepan.

2. Cook for 5 minutes on medium heat.

3. Strain the liquid.

4. Serve.

Preparation time: 10 minutes

Cooking time: 5 minutes

Total time: 15 minutes

Servings: 4

Nutritional Values

- *Calories 187*
- *Total Fat 13 g*
- *Saturated Fat 10.7 g*
- *Cholesterol 0 mg*
- *Sodium 60 mg*
- *Total Carbohydrates 4 g*
- *Dietary Fiber 0 g*
- *Total Sugars 2.5 g*
- *Protein 1.5 g*

Low-Carb Sangria

Ingredients

- ½ cup brandy
- 1 bottle red wine
- 2 tablespoons lemon juice
- 3 tablespoons Swerve
- 1 lemon, thinly sliced

How to prepare

1. Add and mix all the sangria ingredients in a saucepan.

2. Cook for 5 minutes on low heat.

3. Serve.

Preparation time: 10 minutes

Cooking time: 5 minutes

Total time: 15 minutes

Servings: 2

Nutritional Values

- ➤ *Calories 165*
- ➤ *Total Fat 0.3 g*
- ➤ *Saturated Fat 0 g*
- ➤ *Cholesterol 0 mg*
- ➤ *Sodium 4 mg*
- ➤ *Total Carbohydrates 7 g*
- ➤ *Dietary Fiber 3.1 g*
- ➤ *Sugars 0.5 g*
- ➤ *Protein 1.5 g*

Vanilla Tea

Ingredients

- ➢ 1 orange pekoe tea bag
- ➢ 1 cup boiling water
- ➢ 2 tablespoons almond milk
- ➢ 1 teaspoon Swerve
- ➢ ½ teaspoon vanilla extract
- ➢ ½ teaspoon ground cinnamon

How to prepare

1. Add all the tea ingredients to a pan and cook for 5 minutes.
2. Leave them for 5 minutes then strain the liquid.
3. Garnish with cinnamon.
4. Serve.

Preparation time: 10 minutes

Cooking time: 0 minutes

Total time: 10 minutes

Servings: 1

Nutritional Values

➢ *Calories 117*
➢ *Total Fat 3.8 g*
➢ *Saturated Fat 1.2 g*
➢ *Cholesterol 2 mg*
➢ *Sodium 110 mg*
➢ *Total Carbohydrate 6.6 g*
➢ *Dietary Fiber 3 g*
➢ *Sugars 19.4 g*
➢ *Protein 1.7 g*

Fresh Mint Tea

Ingredients

➢ 2 cups of water

➢ 4 fresh mint leaves

How to prepare

1. Add all the tea ingredients to a pan and cook for 5 minutes.

2. Leave them for 5 minutes then strain the liquid.

3. Garnish with mint leaves.

4. Serve.

Preparation time: 10 minutes

Cooking time: 5 minutes

Total time: 15 minutes

Servings: 2

Nutritional Values

- ➢ *Calories 15*
- ➢ *Total Fat 0.1 g*
- ➢ *Saturated Fat 0 g*
- ➢ *Cholesterol 0 mg*
- ➢ *Sodium 0 mg*
- ➢ *Total Carbohydrates 4 g*
- ➢ *Dietary Fiber 0.5 g*
- ➢ *Sugars 3.5 g*
- ➢ *Protein 0.3 g*

Chapter 13: Holiday Keto Cold Drinks (Alcohol/Non-Alcohol)

Mojito

Ingredients

- Juice of 1 lime
- 1 teaspoon granulated sugar

- ➢ Small handful mint leaves
- ➢ 2 ounces white rum
- ➢ Soda water, to taste

How to prepare

1. Blend and mix all the ingredients in a jug.
2. Serve chilled.

Preparation time: 10 minutes
Cooking time: 0 minutes
Total time: 10 minutes
Servings: 1

Nutritional Values

- ➢ *Calories 140*
- ➢ *Total Fat 0.2 g*
- ➢ *Saturated Fat 0 g*
- ➢ *Cholesterol 0 mg*
- ➢ *Sodium 7 mg*
- ➢ *Total Carbohydrates 1.8 g*
- ➢ *Dietary Fiber 1.5 g*
- ➢ *Total Sugars 0 g*
- ➢ *Protein 0.7 g*

Cranberry Prosecco

Ingredients

- ➢ ½ cup Swerve
- ➢ ½ cup fresh cranberries
- ➢ ½ cup cranberry juice
- ➢ 1 bottle Prosecco
- ➢ Sprigs of fresh mint

How to prepare

1. Blend and mix all the ingredients in a cocktail shaker.
2. Serve chilled.

Preparation time: 10 minutes

Cooking time: 0 minutes

Total time: 10 minutes

Servings: 2

Nutritional Values

➢ *Calories 140*

➢ *Total Fat 0.2 g*

➢ *Saturated Fat 0 g*

➢ *Cholesterol 0 mg*

➢ *Sodium 7 mg*

➢ *Total Carbohydrates 1.8 g*

➢ *Dietary Fiber 1.5 g*

➢ *Total Sugars 0 g*

➢ *Protein 0.7 g*

Ginger Mule

Ingredients

- ➢ 4 ounces premium vodka
- ➢ 1 ounce fresh lime juice
- ➢ 1 ounce ginger syrup
- ➢ 8 ounces diet ginger ale
- ➢ Fresh mint leaves to garnish

How to prepare

1. Blend and mix all the ingredients in a cocktail shaker.
2. Strain the mixture into a glass.
3. Serve chilled.

Preparation time: 10 minutes

Cooking time: 0 minutes

Total time: 10 minutes

Servings: 2

Nutritional Values

➢ *Calories 180*

➢ *Total Fat 0 g*

➢ *Saturated Fat 0 g*

➢ *Cholesterol 0 mg*

➢ *Sodium 17 mg*

➢ *Total Carbohydrates 3.1 g*

➢ *Dietary Fiber 0.1 g*

➢ *Total Sugars 0.2 g*

➢ *Protein 0.1 g*

Turmeric Milkshake

Ingredients

- ➢ 13 ounces almond milk
- ➢ 2 tablespoons coconut oil
- ➢ ¾ teaspoon turmeric powder
- ➢ ½ teaspoon ginger powder
- ➢ ¼ teaspoon cinnamon
- ➢ ¼ teaspoon vanilla
- ➢ Granulated Swerve, to taste
- ➢ Pinch Himalayan salt
- ➢ 2 ice cubes

How to prepare

1. Put all the turmeric shake ingredients into a blender jug.
2. Press the pulse button and blend until smooth.
3. Serve.

Preparation time: 10 minutes
Cooking time: 0 minutes
Total time: 10 minutes
Servings: 2

Nutritional Values

- *Calories 343*
- *Total Fat 35.5 g*
- *Saturated Fat 31.8 g*
- *Cholesterol 0 mg*
- *Sodium 19 mg*
- *Total Carbohydrates 7.8 g*
- *Dietary Fiber 3 g*
- *Total Sugars 4.1 g*
- *Protein 2.9 g*

Electrolyte Elixir

Ingredients

- ➢ 8 cups of water
- ➢ 1 teaspoon salt
- ➢ ½ teaspoon magnesium
- ➢ ½ cup lemon juice

How to prepare

1. Mix juice, salt, magnesium, and lemon juice in a pitcher.
2. Serve.

Preparation time: 10 minutes
Cooking time: 0 minutes
Total time: 10 minutes
Servings: 8

Nutritional Values

➢ *Calories 4*
➢ *Total Fat 0.1 g*
➢ *Saturated Fat 0.1 g*
➢ *Cholesterol 0 mg*
➢ *Sodium 301 mg*
➢ *Total Carbohydrates 0.3 g*
➢ *Dietary Fiber 0.1 g*
➢ *Total Sugars 0.3 g*
➢ *Protein 0.1 g*

Cinnamon Coffee

Ingredients

- ➤ 2 tablespoons ground coffee
- ➤ 1 teaspoon ground cinnamon
- ➤ 2 cups of water
- ➤ 1/3 cup heavy whipping cream

How to prepare

1. Put all the cinnamon coffee ingredients into a blender jug.

2. Press the pulse button and blend until smooth.

3. Serve.

Preparation time: 10 minutes

Cooking time: 0 minutes

Total time: 10 minutes

Servings: 2

Nutritional Values

- ➢ *Calories 72*
- ➢ *Total Fat 7.4 g*
- ➢ *Saturated Fat 4.6 g*
- ➢ *Cholesterol 27 mg*
- ➢ *Sodium 15 mg*
- ➢ *Total Carbohydrates 1.5 g*
- ➢ *Dietary Fiber 0.6 g*
- ➢ *Total Sugars 0 g*
- ➢ *Protein 0.5 g*

Iced Tea

Ingredients

➢ 1 cup of cold water

➢ 1 cup green tea, brewed

➢ 1 cup of ice cubes

How to prepare

1. Put all the iced tea into a blender jug.

2. Press the pulse button and blend until smooth.

3. Serve.

Preparation time: 10 minutes

Cooking time: 0 minutes

Total time: 10 minutes

Servings: 2

Nutritional Values

➢ *Calories 48*

➢ *Total Fat 0 g*

➢ *Saturated Fat 0 g*

➢ *Cholesterol 0 mg*

➢ *Sodium 15 mg*

➢ *Total Carbohydrates 1 g*

➢ *Dietary Fiber 0.8 g*

➢ *Sugars 0.2 g*

➢ *Protein 0.1 g*

Strawberry Smoothie

Ingredients

- ➢ ¼ cup heavy whipping cream
- ➢ ¾ cup unsweetened almond milk
- ➢ 2 teaspoons granulated erythritol
- ➢ 4 ounces of frozen strawberries
- ➢ ½ cup ice
- ➢ ½ teaspoon vanilla extract

How to prepare

1. Put all the strawberry smoothie ingredients into a

blender jug.

2. Press the pulse button and blend until smooth.

3. Serve.

Preparation time: 10 minutes

Cooking time: 0 minutes

Total time: 10 minutes

Servings: 2

Nutritional Values

- ➢ *Calories 165*
- ➢ *Total Fat 2 g*
- ➢ *Saturated Fat 1.2 g*
- ➢ *Cholesterol 0 mg*
- ➢ *Sodium 5 mg*
- ➢ *Total Carbohydrates 4 g*
- ➢ *Dietary Fiber 1.4 g*
- ➢ *Sugars 0.7 g*
- ➢ *Protein 0.6 g*

Blueberry Smoothie

Ingredients

- ➤ 1 cup blueberries
- ➤ 1 (8-ounce) container plain yogurt
- ➤ ¾ cup almond milk
- ➤ 2 tablespoons Swerve
- ➤ ½ teaspoon vanilla extract
- ➤ ⅛ teaspoon ground nutmeg

How to prepare

1. Put all the blueberry smoothie ingredients into a blender jug.
2. Press the pulse button and blend until smooth.
3. Serve.

Preparation time: 10 minutes

Cooking time: 0 minutes

Total time: 10 minutes

Servings: 2

Nutritional Values

- ➢ *Calories 178*
- ➢ *Total Fat 10 g*
- ➢ *Saturated Fat 3.4 g*
- ➢ *Cholesterol 134 mg*
- ➢ *Sodium 23 mg*
- ➢ *Total Carbohydrates 4 g*
- ➢ *Dietary Fiber 0.2 g*
- ➢ *Sugars 0.1 g*
- ➢ *Protein 0.8 g*

Ginger Spinach Smoothie

Ingredients

- ⅓ cup coconut milk
- ⅔ cup water
- 2 tablespoons lime juice
- 1 ounce frozen spinach
- 2 teaspoons fresh ginger, grated

How to prepare

1. Add all the ginger smoothie ingredients to a high-speed blender.

2. Press the pulse button and blend until smooth.

3. Serve.

Preparation time: 10 minutes

Cooking time: 0 minutes

Total time: 10 minutes

Servings: 2

Nutritional Values

- ➤ *Calories 112*
- ➤ *Total Fat 12.6 g*
- ➤ *Saturated Fat 17.4 g*
- ➤ *Cholesterol 0 mg*
- ➤ *Sodium 18 mg*
- ➤ *Total Carbohydrates 2.3 g*
- ➤ *Dietary Fiber 1.8 g*
- ➤ *Sugars 0.5 g*
- ➤ *Protein 1 g*

Conclusion

If you are on a ketogenic diet and want to optimize your carb intake on all the special holidays, then the above-mentioned recipes can help you create a diversified menu. These recipes are created for all holiday celebrations. Here you can find flavorsome turkey roasting ideas for Thanksgiving and casserole-making secrets for the Christmas celebrations. From special drinks to desserts, you can have it all on your holiday menu. We know the struggle of every ketogenic dieter; hence, we bring them the best ways to reduce their carb intake while enjoying the same flavors and aromas as others do on these special days. So, give these recipes a try and share them with your loved ones to spread the joy and warmth of all the holidays. And if you find this cookbook interesting and helpful, then you can always gift the book to your friends and family to spread the holiday magic around!

Made in the USA
Las Vegas, NV
28 November 2022

60435569R20177